Henri's Mantle

D0253474

Also by CHRIS GLASER

Uncommon Calling

Come Home!

Coming Out to God

The Word Is Out

Unleashed! The Wit and Wisdom of Calvin the Dog

Coming Out As Sacrament

Communion of Life

Reformation of the Heart

VISIT
www.ChrisGlaser.com

E-MAIL
ChrsGlaser@aol.com

Henri's Mantle

100 MEDITATIONS ON NOUWEN'S LEGACY

Chris Glaser

THE PILGRIM PRESS   CLEVELAND

The Pilgrim Press, 700 Prospect Avenue, Cleveland, Ohio 44115-1100
pilgrimpress.com
Copyright © 2002 by Chris R. Glaser

Printed in the United States of America on acid-free paper

07   06   05   04   03   02   5   4   3   2   1

Library of Congress Cataloging-in-Publication Data
Glaser, Chris.
     Henri's mantle : 100 meditations on Nouwen's legacy /
Chris Glaser.
          p.   cm.
     Includes bibliographical references
     ISBN 0-8298-1497-3 (pbk. : alk. paper)
     1. Nouwen, Henri J. M.—Meditations.   I. Title.

BX4705.N87 G53   2002
242—dc21

2002029073

IN THANKSGIVING TO GOD

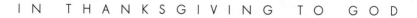

for John Ballew and Erin Swenson,
friends who got me through "the recent unpleasantness,"

and for Wade Jones,
making better times still better.

CONTENTS

Contents

Contents

In biblical terms, *mantle* is the equivalent of *legacy*. As he was swept away into the heavens, Elijah's mantle fell on Elisha, who received a double share of Elijah's spirit, as he had prayed. Both served as prophetic voices to their cultures, reminding their people of God and God's hope for them.

Henri J. M. Nouwen's mantle includes more than forty books on cultivating a spiritual life, "the inner voice of love." This Dutch-born Roman Catholic priest wrote them during his years teaching at Notre Dame, Yale, and Harvard, and during his ministries alongside the poor in Latin America and the disabled of the L'Arche community in Toronto. Since his death in 1996, his mantle has been passed to all who read and reflect on his work—Catholic, Protestant, Orthodox, and unchurched alike. His spirit is multiplied many times over in the millions of readers who take his words about the God of love to heart. It is what Henri called the "fruitfulness" that may be harvested only after our brief lifespans.

I was first a student and then a friend of Henri's over a span of a quarter of a century. His death at the relatively early age of sixty-four years sent a shock wave through the spiritual community. Many of us dealt with our grief by gathering not only for his funeral mass, but for further reflection on his legacy. I began conducting retreats about Henri's life and work, not so much to analyze his opus, but to extend it in the lives of those familiar and unfamiliar with his work.

Though the spirituality of Jesus was the foundation for Henri's writing, its cornerstone was Henri's own vulnerability, his willingness to share intimately his own spiritual struggle. He believed that the Christian was called to be for others *The Wounded Healer*, the name of his most influential early work.

What I've found remarkable as I've brought people together to consider Henri's legacy is that, almost from the start of a workshop or retreat, these strangers to each other readily reveal intimacies to one another. This may be Henri's greatest legacy, that he transforms strangers to lovers—that is, breaks down protective walls and superficial distractions to reveal open hearts, wounded and blessed, yearning to love and be loved. The transformation of strangers to lovers, I believe, is the proper role of spirituality.

Though Henri's base was Christian spirituality and community, his message and his understanding was inclusive of those who follow different spiritual paths. That, too, in my view, reflects the depth of true spirituality, which acknowledges that even religious differences may detract and distract from the good and from God, whose unitive essence breaks down all differentiation, even religious division.

I refer to him as Henri because that's how he wanted to be known, much as his fellow Dutchman and one of his favorite artists, Vincent van Gogh, simply signed his paintings "Vincent." In one of his books, he goes so far as to say the initials "J. M." in the middle of his name could stand for "Just Me."

I feel presumptuous writing this book. There are many who knew Henri better than I did. There are many who teach Henri better than I can. But, in the same spirit in which I offer the retreats on him, I offer these meditations on his words and life in the hopes that his ministry will continue to proliferate. Just as the loaves and fishes blessed by Jesus fed a multitude, so Henri's words, blessed by Jesus and the Spirit, may find fertile soil within our hearts to bear fruit that will feed multitudes seeking spiritual food.

That is his greatest legacy, a double share of his spirit.

Chris Glaser
Atlanta

I kept refusing to hear the voice
that speaks from the very depth of my being
and says: "You are my Beloved, on you my favor
rests." That voice has always been there, but it
seems that I was much more eager to listen to
other, louder voices saying: "Prove that you
are worth something; do something relevant,
spectacular or powerful, and then you
will earn the love you so desire.

Life of the Beloved, 28–29

Henri wrote these words in a book written at the suggestion of a young friend who told him that a kind of "generic" book on spirituality was needed for those who didn't speak the "in" language of any faith tradition. Henri always felt a burden for outsiders because he himself felt like an outsider. He distilled the essence of Christianity in *Life of the Beloved:* that, with Jesus, we must hear God's affirmation, "You are my beloved child, with whom I am well pleased." It was something Henri longed to really "hear" himself.

He candidly reports in the book that when he showed the manuscript to his friend, the young man responded that it didn't quite hit the mark. Of course, Henri published it anyway! Perhaps the book didn't fit the request because it was hard for Henri to be other than Christian in his outlook on life.

When we say we are "preaching to the choir," it's worth pointing out that the choir may not be fully converted. Even if *Life of the Beloved* didn't reach those outside the Christian faith, it still speaks to those of us who are not fully converted, fully able to hear that inner voice that calls us Beloved. When I first saw the book I bought it for a friend just graduating from seminary and going to serve his first parish. The friend was dealing with issues of identity and openness, and I did not want him to forget himself in his service to others. He needed to remind himself that he, too, is the Beloved.

In *The Living Reminder*, Henri writes that the minister, which he viewed as *every* Christian, is the living reminder of Christ for others. "The great vocation of the minister is to continuously make connections between the human story and the divine story," he wrote (*The Living Reminder*, 24). To do this, Christians who want to serve others must develop a spiritual life that reminds them of their belovedness so we can "distinguish service from our need to be liked, praised, or respected" (*The Living Reminder*, 30).

Like many ministers, Henri preached what he wanted to practice. Visiting a retreat center run by a monastic community, I overheard a brother of the order say acerbically about Henri, "I wish he would stop *writing* about wanting to pray, and just *pray*!" Like the ultimate priest depicted in Hebrews, in Henri "we have one who in every respect has been tested as we are" and therefore can "sympathize with our weaknesses" (Hebrews 4:15) when it comes to developing our spiritual center.

Key to the popularity of Henri's writings is that he had not "arrived." Being in prayer itself, he writes, is "being useless in God's presence" and letting God "speak in the silence of my heart" (*Living Reminder*, 52). In this place, we are reminded of our belovedness rather than our usefulness. And from this place, God may speak through us to others.

༄ I AM YOUR BELOVED CHILD, GOD, WITH WHOM YOU ARE WELL PLEASED.

The clowns don't have it together,
they do not succeed in what they try, they are
awkward, out of balance, and left-handed,
but . . . they are on our side. . . . Of the
virtuosi we say, "How can they do it?"
Of the clowns we say, "They are like us."

Clowning in Rome — Reflections on Solitude,
Celibacy, Prayer, and Contemplation, 2, 110

Henri would have made a fine clown. His large, flapping hands, tall, gangly body, and basic bodily awkwardness would have lent itself well to the exaggerated gestures, dramatic posturing, and comic pratfalls required in that profession. Once he brought Ken Feit, a Jesuit-turned-clown, to Yale Divinity School for a two-week stint as an artist-in-residence. In the midst of scientific graduate work at Berkeley years before, while studying a textbook on the steps of the science building there, Ken's imagination had been captured not by his text but by a spider weaving an intricate web above his head. This quirky conversion experience prompted him to leave an intended career in science and go to clown school. What the world needed was not another scientist, especially not another mathematician, but another clown.

As Henri lectured one day in class, Ken came forward, silently, throwing Henri off center. With a quizzical smile on his face, Henri asked, "Oh, do you want to take over the class?" Ken assumed Henri's place behind the lectern and mimed the rest of the lecture, waving his hands in typical Henri patterns, leaning over the podium like a turtle stretching its head out of its shell in Henri's characteristic way of making a point, scrunching his face to find the absolutely perfect words to reveal some truth of the spiritual life, all in silence. Ken made Henri laugh; he made us all laugh. All that we did in that class, soberly titled "Discipline and Discipleship," was placed in perspective. God made us to have fun, too. God also made us to have fun with ourselves, not taking ourselves more seriously than we ought, remembering that the spiritual life is one marginalized by a society whose preoccupation with material pursuits and the supposed "reality" of fame and fortune made our ministries and our prayers seem insubstantial and inconsequential.

And yet, as laughter is necessary to survive and to celebrate, so being "fools for Christ" brings salvation and sacrament to others.

꙾ GOD, SAVE US FROM OUR SILLY SERIOUSNESS AND BLESS US WITH YOUR SACRED LAUGHTER.

I experience deep sorrow that I have not
become who I wanted to be, and that the
God to whom I have prayed so much has
not given me what I have most desired.

Can You Drink the Cup? 34

Henri's melancholy, captured in this sentence, is the truth of
almost everyone's life. Henri's way of being disarmingly hon-
est about the deficiencies in his own life unveils the reality
that few of us can truthfully say that we have achieved, even
for ourselves alone, what we had hoped. And almost all of us
can name a variety of circumstances in which God has not
answered our prayers.

I am suspicious of those who, toward the end of their
lives, claim to have no regrets. I can't imagine getting through
life without regretting choices, decisions, behaviors, directions, ignorance, missteps, and mistakes. I've also doubted
those who claimed to "have it all together," or whose faith
gives them a smug self-satisfaction. Lillian Hellman wrote of
herself as an "unfinished woman," and *if we are still alive,*
there is always the sense of being unfinished. If death is the
only thing that finishes us off, then we have been fully alive
up until the last moment.

In his book, *People of the Lie,* therapist Scott Peck charac-
terizes evil as "the unquestioned self." Though one may become saintly to a fault, doubting the self so much that pro-
crastination, indecision, and inaction become the rule of life,
still, those of us who are certain of our rectitude may be most
resistant to the changes required to do the right thing in a set

of circumstances for which our preconceptions (or prejudices) have not prepared us. That was, I believe, what Jesus rejected about the law of his ancestors as practiced: such codification can paralyze the heart and limit the Spirit. His responses to the self-righteous Pharisees did not demean that law but diminished its absolute authority. We are always going to be saved by God's love, not by God's law. Thus we live by God's grace, not by our own perfection or sense of completion.

And, Henri points out in *Our Greatest Gift*, our work is not even completed during our short lifespan. God continues to bless our efforts in what Henri called "the fruitfulness of death," that is, the spiritual harvest resulting from a lifetime of giving ourselves to others. Remember the film *It's a Wonderful Life*, and how the protagonist George Bailey discovered what would have happened had he not lived. We do not always know the reverberations of the smallest of good deeds, and as the plaque in the office of the Bailey Savings & Loan reads, "What we take with us is that which we give away." The title of Henri's book parallels the title of the short story by Philip Van Doren Stern on which the Frank Capra film was based, "The Greatest Gift." With his positive yet firm grip on the human condition, Henri could be the spiritual Frank Capra!

ℭ **PERFECT GOD**, PRESERVE MY LIFE BY PROVIDING ME WITH NEW OPPORTUNITIES TO STRETCH MYSELF, REFORM MYSELF, AND BE RESURRECTED TO FRESH POSSIBILITIES.

Somewhere we know that without a lonely place
our lives are in danger. Somewhere we know that
without silence words lose their meaning, that without listening speaking no longer heals, that
without distance closeness cannot cure.

Out of Solitude, 14

Writing about the ancient monastics of the desert in *The Way of the Heart*, Henri suggests that we each might fashion a kind of wilderness for ourselves, a place and time *set apart* (the literal meaning of *holy*) to pray, not simply offering words to God, but offering silence. In the makeshift chapel Henri put together shortly after his arrival at Daybreak, the L'Arche community in Toronto, he and I sat for a solid hour contemplating the host (the wafered "body of Christ") in the very early morning hours. I enjoy silence, but not in such wide swathes, without benefit of reading or writing materials. It was remarkable to me that Henri, known for his restlessness, could light in one place and achieve silence for such a period of time. Indeed, he did fidget now and again, and I'm sure his head was "jabbering like a banana tree of monkeys," a favorite phrase he used in his presentations to depict the constant noise in our minds that keeps us from the focus and attentiveness of the spiritual life.

Out of Solitude consists of three sermons Henri gave at Yale's Battell Chapel on three consecutive Sundays in 1973. He created them on retreat at Mercy Center along the shores of Long Island Sound. One weekend I too retreated there with him. I had just arranged for a major speaker at the

Divinity School, one that brought attention to my own quiet activism there, and it had been an emotional "coming out" for me. After so many words, struggling to have the speaker invited, preventing the withdrawal of the invitation, listening to his remarks and the dialogue it sparked among the hundred students who attended, having conversations with many as a result of his presentation, I was in need of the healing that only silence and distance can provide.

Henri asked me to read and comment on the sermon he was working on that weekend. It says something about his attentiveness to his students that something I said found its way into the sermon, quoted as "a student from California," and that he thanked me by giving me my first signed copy when the sermon was published as a chapter in the book the following year.

Thus began for me a series of personal retreats that refreshed me in my activism, in my ministry, and in my relationships. As Henri could listen on personal retreat to one of his hundreds of "groupies"—me—I have been better able to listen for God, to myself, and to others. It has not made me a perfect person, minister, friend, lover, let alone a mystic, but it has made me a little better than I otherwise would have been.

ᗤ AFTER I THINK ON THESE THINGS, LET MY THOUGHTS AND THESE WORDS SUBSIDE, SUBMERGING FROM MIND TO HEART, FROM ARTICULATION TO FEELING, FROM CLARIFICATION TO EMBODIED WILL, FROM THINKING TO BEING, FROM SOUND TO SILENCE.

> People will constantly try to hook
> your wounded self. They will point out
> your needs, your character defects, your
> limitations and sins. That is how they
> attempt to dismiss what God, through
> you, is saying to them.

The Inner Voice of Love, 99

Though Henri's most familiar concept is the minister as the wounded healer, presented in one of his earliest books, titled *The Wounded Healer,* the liabilities of woundedness became apparent to him in this latter epistle of the heart, written during an emotional and spiritual breakdown in the face of unrequited love. As already noted, Henri used the term minister for all Christians; thus he felt all Christians were called as wounded healers. With the messianic figure in an ancient rabbinic story, we are to unbind and rebandage our wounds one at a time so we may yet be available to bind other's wounds. And with the crucified and resurrected Christ, we offer our lives for others, wounds and all.

In his books, Henri offered his life for others; he unbound personal wounds one at a time to demonstrate the healing God can bring. From his self-perceived pettiness to his desperate loneliness, Henri manifested the human condition in which we all participate. More than that, he demonstrated how airing those wounds in God's presence through prayer, community, and ministry proved healing to self and world.

But he was "accused" of not having a life experience he did not write about, he once told me, as was said of Thomas

9

Merton, "He never had an unpublished thought." "So?" I wonder, "What else do we have to write about? Even our thoughts reflecting on research, or our imagination in fiction, are ultimately always words about ourselves."

I was once coleading a retreat with a biblical and antiquities scholar who made an intriguing academic presentation. But it was when participants asked her for her own story that the audience was captivated and transformed.

Saint Augustine recognized, in his *Confessions*, that telling our stories reveals the divine at work, the *imago dei* imprinted in human experience. His book gave birth to a new genre in literature, the personal memoir. Autobiography has become yet one more avenue in religious literature for doing theology, especially practical or applied theology, from Augustine to Simone Weil, from Teresa of Avila and John of the Cross to Etty Hillesum and Thomas Merton.

Thus, my story and your story are important conduits for the proclamation of the gospel. Those who try to dismiss the good news we proclaim because of our weaknesses, inadequacies, and sins are the same who taunted and mocked Jesus of Nazareth on the cross: "He saved others; let him save himself if he is the Messiah of God, [God's] chosen one!" (Luke 23:35).

ɶ NOT WHAT GOES INTO OUR HEARTS DEFILES, BUT WHAT COMES OUT OF OUR HEARTS. NOT SIMPLY LIFE EXPERIENCE IS SPIRITUALLY IMPORTANT, BUT HOW THAT EXPERIENCE IS TRANSFORMED IN OUR SERVICE TO LOVE IS VITAL AND ETERNAL.

> You are confronted again and again with
> the choice of letting God speak or letting your
> wounded self cry out. . . . When you let your
> wounded self express itself in the form of apolo-
> gies, arguments, or complaints—through which it
> cannot be truly heard—you will only grow
> frustrated and increasingly feel rejected.
>
> *The Inner Voice of Love,* 99

Henri wrote this at the end of a promising new relationship. He often said that those we hurt most and those who hurt us most are those closest and dearest to us. Such was the case when a member of his community to whom he had opened the deepest desires of his heart pulled away from him, feeling unable to meet Henri's expectations of the friendship.

I avidly read the journal when it was published, because it was released on the very day of Henri's death from a heart attack in September of 1996. It was a parting message from someone I considered not only a friend, but an informal spiritual director. Admittedly I was curious as to just how revealing it would be. But I found just enough distancing from the personal to make its message more universally realized. Henri credited editors, students, and friends with helping him in his writings to differentiate from what's personal and what's private, what's universal and what's "just me," even as he practiced Carl Rogers's truth: "What is personal is most general" or universal.

What Henri captures in his words is an experience common to many in failed, intimate relationships. When I subsequently had a similar experience in the ending of a long-term relationship, I reread *The Inner Voice of Love* during my morning prayer time to remind myself that I was loved, beloved, even lovable. Over the course of that year I reread it three times!

Henri knew that rejection from those we allow close recalls the fear we all hold that if people *really* knew us, they wouldn't love us. At the end of my own relationship, that's exactly what I felt. I felt that my fears had been confirmed, that I truly was not worthy of love. Worse than not receiving love is the belief that we are not lovable. That leads to unnecessary apologies for who we are, unneeded arguments for why we need someone's love, and unheeded whining about being unloved and unlovable.

"Since that deep place in you where your identity as a child of God is rooted has been unknown to you for a long time, those who were able to touch you there had a sudden and often overwhelming power over you," Henri wrote (*Inner Voice,* 70). All of Henri's yearnings for love—whether from God or Jesus or others—implied his fear of being unlovable. And yet, at the core of his yearning, he recognized that he—and each of us—was already the Beloved. The spiritual life is the means of accessing this realization, cultivating that "inner voice of love." It was this recognition, Henri believed, that transformed Jesus at his baptism into the prophet and minister he became: "You are my Son, the Beloved; with you I am well pleased" (Mark 1:11). This could be viewed as Jesus' enlightenment—if you will, his "conversion" experience.

Speaking from our wounded selves, we speak from our fear of being unlovable. Letting God speak through us, we speak from our assurance that each of us is a beloved child of God.

ᗡ **WITH BOLDNESS WE CLAIM OUR BELOVEDNESS. WE ARE WOUNDED, BUT NOT FATALLY OR FATALISTICALLY. FOR WE ARE BLESSED WITH A LOVE THAT CREATES AND REDEEMS AND SUSTAINS US.**

The Flying Rodleighs are trapeze
artists who perform in the German circus
Simoneit-Barum. . . . I will never forget how
enraptured I became when I first saw the
Rodleighs move through the air, flying and
catching as elegant dancers.

Our Greatest Gift, 66

So enraptured was Henri that he visited the Rodleighs backstage and subsequently accepted an invitation to travel with them for a number of weeks. In a presentation videotaped on May 5, 1994, by the L'Arche community of Mobile, Alabama, he explains that, in watching the Rodleighs, he had finally found his true vocation! *Angels Over the Net,* a documentary for television in his native Holland, captures him laughing that, in telling others about his newfound love, his heavily-accented English and his listeners' expectations led them to confuse "trapeze" with "Trappist."

The spiritual seeker who tried and wrote about two prolonged visits in the Trappist monastery of the Genesee Valley now wanted to become a trapeze artist! The spiritual writer who early in his career in *Clowning in Rome,* described ministers as clowns rather than "the virtuosi," toward the end of his life took copious notes for a book he never wrote connecting the spiritual life with the high-flying Rodleighs!

But this is not quite the contradiction it seems. The awkward Henri who once identified with pratfalling clowns wistfully wished for the strength and the grace to fly through the air. And the exhilaration and excitement he experienced seeing trapeze artists risking double and triple jumps paralleled his and his listeners' own exhilaration and excitement whenever he made a presentation on the spiritual life. He virtually did double and triple jumps trying to get his message across.

"As a flyer," the leader of the Rodleigh troupe told Henri, "I must have complete trust in my catcher. The public might think that I am the great star of the trapeze, but the real star is Joe, my catcher. He has to be there for me with split-second precision and grab me out of the air as I come to him in the long jump. . . . The secret is that the flyer does nothing and the catcher does everything. . . . The worst thing the flyer can do is try to catch the catcher. . . . If I grabbed Joe's wrists, I might break them, or he might break mine, and that would be the end for both of us. . . . The flyer must trust, with outstretched arms, that his catcher will be there for him" (*Our Greatest Gift*, 66–67).

In *Our Greatest Gift*, Henri uses this as a metaphor for dying: trusting God, "the catcher." But for Henri it meant so much more. Many years before, his spiritual guide at the Trappist monastery of the Genesee, John Eudes Bamberger, had told him to trust the Spirit more in his work, pointing out that in everything he did, he acted as if his whole life and reputation depended on it. In 1982, at the Quaker retreat center Pendle Hill outside Philadelphia, Henri passed on the same advice to me, knowing I tended to overly prepare and thus tense up in speaking engagements: "Trust the Spirit more," he advised.

༚ IN LIVING AND IN DYING, O GOD, GIVE ME THE FAITH TO TRUST YOU, THE CATCHER. "LORD, I BELIEVE; HELP MY UNBELIEF!"

Fear not only prevents intimacy; it also
thwarts fecundity. When fear dominates our
lives, we cannot quietly and patiently protect
that holy space where fruit can grow.
Two ways in which fear manifests itself
are sterility and productivity.

*Lifesigns: Intimacy, Fecundity, and
Ecstasy in Christian Perspective,* 57

Had Henri been a less productive person, the reader might be tempted to dismiss this as a saying to defend idleness, a special pleading for someone who fails to produce. But the fact that he churned out more than forty books in less than forty years of ministry—not to mention speeches, sermons, correspondence, notes for abandoned as well as future books, and his everyday work as a priest—gives greater weight to this insight.

And, had Henri been a less admittedly fearful person, those of us afraid of so many things might not prove as receptive to his warning. If Henri "had it all together," his "Be not afraid!" imperatives might ring less true. If Henri were an angel whose very presence was that of God, like the ones who appeared for Jesus' nativity or at the empty tomb, we might say "it's easy for *him* to say" when adjuring us mere mortals to trust.

As my own father faced death, he offered his fears alongside his faith, making his faith all the more potent. Henri described a similar mix of faith and doubt in his own father's response to a radio interviewer's question about the afterlife: "When I die, well, then we will see!" (*Our Greatest Gift,* 110).

The same mix of fear and faith was true of my spiritual "father," Henri. At times his anxiety and fear led to sterile periods in which he felt unable to fulfill his ministry. At other times he produced books that had little new to say. The gently chiding joke among his friends was that Henri wrote the same book forty times! Henri himself told me that his publishers wanted manuscripts he felt were far too short.

I left an editorial position in Los Angeles when I moved to Atlanta. Without a job, I literally had to "publish or perish." So I took on an intimidating request from my publisher I had been resisting: a book of meditations for every day of the year. And I was given only three and a half months to write it! Reporting my progress to my editor, I would joke, "I'm meditating as fast as I can!" In that case, fear of having no income made me quite fertile.

I sent a copy to Henri. He wrote that he had tried such a volume, but gave up after ninety entries. He feared he didn't have it in him to produce more. When they were published as *Here and Now*, he sent me a copy with the inscription, "This book was meant to contain also 365 daily meditations, but after ninety I gave up!" Only toward the end of his life did he produce such a book in *Bread for the Journey*. Its daily entries are casual and relaxed, not as intense and complex as *Here and Now*. Henri had nothing to prove.

"When fear dominates our lives, we cannot quietly and patiently protect that holy space where fruit can grow," Henri wrote. "Perfect love casts out all fear," affirms 1 John 4:18. The holy space where fruit can grow is God's sanctuary of perfect love.

༄ As I REST, LISTEN, BREATHE, AND WAIT IN YOUR LOVE, O GOD, MAY MY FEAR SUBSIDE THAT I HAVE NOTHING TO GIVE, AS MY FAITH GROWS THAT I HAVE NOTHING TO PROVE.

We can only celebrate if there is
something present that can be celebrated.
We cannot celebrate Christmas where there is
nothing new born here and now, we cannot
celebrate Easter when no new life becomes
visible, we cannot celebrate Pentecost when
there is no Spirit whatsoever to celebrate.

Creative Ministry, 93

Many if not most of us can remember a Christmas when we felt more like Scrooge than Tiny Tim, an Easter on which we identified with doubting Thomas rather than the joyful Mary, a Pentecost at which we mocked those "filled with the Spirit" rather than giving ourselves over to the Spirit's power.

The Christian calendar is given us to remind us of the seasons and high points of our faith. If we are "unseasonable" or feeling low, we may feel hypocritical or unfaithful. On top of that, every Sunday worship is intended to celebrate God's resurrection (thus vindication) of Jesus on that first Easter Sunday. Few of us are *always* ready to so celebrate!

Henri's words from *Creative Ministry* relieve us from the burden we may feel when our feelings don't match the celebratory nature of our faith. We may be suffering the loss of a loved one, a vocation, a home, our health, or employment—anything dear and vital to us. We may be dealing with feelings of ennui, boredom, hopelessness, fear, anxiety, or anger that are not easily explained, let alone resolved. We may even be satisfied and content, but not quite up to a "party," whether social or ecclesiastical.

But Henri's words also challenge us to hear the angels at the nativity and of the resurrected Christ saying to us, "Fear not!" They challenge us to listen to the message of goodwill to all human beings in the incarnation, the ultimate hope that leads beyond our many losses in the resurrection, and the proclamation of the gospel of God's reign in our own language at Pentecost. And finally, Henri's words challenge us to hear the promise that Christ will be with us to the end of the age.

A problem with "common public worship" is that true worship is uncommon and very personal. To the woman at the well, whose people, the Samaritans, believed in a different worship form and site than his own people, Jesus said, "Woman, believe me, the hour is coming when you will worship [God] neither on this mountain nor in Jerusalem. . . . God is spirit, and those who worship [God] must worship in spirit and truth" (John 4:21, 24).

That, for Henri, requires personal spiritual discipline: a prayer life, shaping a desert for ourselves alongside the ancient Desert Fathers and Mothers, in which we can attend to that still small voice with which God speaks to our world and to us. "Common public worship" requires uncommon, personal effort.

No matter the ebb and flow of Henri's moods from day to day, he gratefully celebrated the Eucharist every day of his ordained life. He taught that gratitude is an approach to life more than a feeling. To give thanks even when all seems against us is part of our discipleship.

ᴄᴡ **Dᴇᴀʀ Gᴏᴅ, ᴡʜᴇɴ I ʟᴀᴄᴋ ᴘᴜʀᴘᴏsᴇ ᴀɴᴅ ᴘᴀssɪᴏɴ, ɢɪᴠᴇ ᴍᴇ ᴠɪsɪᴏɴ ᴀɴᴅ ᴘᴏᴡᴇʀ.**

There was a time when I said:
"Next year I will finally have it together,"
or "When I grow more mature these moments
of inner darkness will go," or "Age will diminish my emotional needs." But now I know that
my sorrows are mine and will not leave me.

Can You Drink the Cup? 33–34

This reflection, coming toward the end of Henri's life, reveals a deeper reality that perhaps only age can bring. It appears in a deceptively simple book that reveals heretofore hidden autobiographical information, from table etiquette of the Nouwen household when Henri was a child to the changing nature of the "table etiquette" of the Eucharist during the forty-year span of Henri's priesthood.

This is also a reflection that resonates most strongly for those of us who are ourselves older, who have lost mothers and fathers, lovers and friends, dreams and desires. Our prayers to hold on to loved ones or to realize our dreams have not always been answered positively, and we may even doubt God. The more idealistic or positive among us may too easily reply that God's response to our requests is sometimes "no," without being fully attentive to our pain, our anguish, our despair. It also contradicts much of what we learn about God's nature in the Bible, who chooses life for us and wants us to love and to know that we are the Beloved. The God of Christianity is a God of Yes (see the apostle Paul on that one in 2 Corinthians 1:19–20).

Jesus said in the Sermon on the Mount, "Is there anyone among you who, if your child asks for bread, will give a stone? Or if the child asks for a fish, will give a snake? If you then, who are evil, know how to give good gifts to your children, how much more will your Father in heaven give good things to those who ask. . . !" (Matthew 7:7–11).

The contradiction of these positive statements and our negative experiences is not easily resolved, glossed over, or ignored. Yet there is a response. Trust. Trust God. Trust God *anyway*. The One who has evolved life itself and the human race in particular and given us loved ones and dreams would seem to have our best interests at heart.

Henri also writes in *Can You Drink the Cup?* "Mostly we are willing to look back at our lives and say, 'I am grateful for the good things that brought me to this place.' But when we lift our cup to life, we must dare to say: 'I am grateful for all that has happened to me and led me to this moment.' . . . When we are crushed like grapes, we cannot think of the wine we will become" (*Can You Drink the Cup?* 74–75, 49).

Trusting God does not make the crushing experiences of our lives less painful, just more hopeful.

∾ OH LORD, I TRUST! BUT HELP MY LACK OF TRUST!

We will never fully understand
the meaning of the sacramental signs
of bread and wine when they do not
make us realize that the whole of nature
is a sacrament pointing to a reality
far beyond itself.

Creative Ministry, 103

In retreats I sometimes invite participants to think about their morning ritual, offering my own as an example. I say "Thank you, God, for another day of life," then pet my dogs (and nudge them off the bed), stretch, splash water on my face, dress, brew coffee, feed the dogs, eat my own breakfast, read the paper, listen to the news on TV, and finally do my morning prayers, usually outside. I greet the morning utilizing every one of my senses: hearing, touch, smell, taste, and sight. But also, it is through the senses that the morning greets me.

A sacrament is a sacred ritual. It is a ritual in which we greet God, but it is also a ritual in which God greets us. And sacraments are sensual in nature. They remind us that our spirituality is not an "out-of-body" experience, but something that happens very much within our bodies. Sacraments are ways in which God touches us with TLC—tender, loving care.

I share Henri's view that all of nature is a sacrament pointing beyond itself to the one who organized chaos, shaped it into being, animated it with purpose, and breathed life into it. When one realizes that all of nature is sacramental—in other words, reveals the sacred, or God, it is easier to embrace the particular sacramental nature of the Eucharist.

Early Christians observed as many as 150 sacraments, later narrowed down to seven, the symbolic number of completeness. For them, all of life was sacramental.

We get into trouble when we fail to recognize the sacred nature of creation and of creatures. We might borrow from our Hindu sisters and brothers the greeting "namustai"—the sacred in me greets the sacred in you. That is, after all, the meaning of passing the Peace of Christ: it is acknowledging in a hug, kiss, or handshake that in Christ we belong to one another and to God.

Henri spent the last decade of his life as chaplain to Daybreak, the L'Arche community for the disabled in Toronto. He served as an assistant to Adam, a disabled man who did not speak. In the posthumous book *Adam: God's Beloved,* Henri wrote of Adam as an incarnation of God's coming to us. The "Christ event" happened for Henri "every time spirit greets spirit in the body" (*Adam: God's Beloved,* 54).

OPEN MY EYES, THAT I MAY SEE, GLIMPSES OF YOUR DIVINITY! MAY THE SACRED IN ME GREET THE SACRED IN OTHERS, KNOWING THAT WE, TOO, ARE OF ONE SUBSTANCE WITH YOU, MOTHER AND FATHER OF US ALL.

But in the midst of this lively and colorful
conglomeration of houses, people, and cars,
there are the domes of Rome pointing to the
places set apart for the Holy One. The churches
of Rome are like beautiful frames around empty
spaces witnessing to [God] who is the quiet,
still center of all human life.

Clowning in Rome, 37

Henri speaks of the need for cathedrals in a city to remind residents to take time for the inner life and for God. Henri is speaking to those of religious vocation, and how their vocations serve as similar reminders to others. But whether ours is religious vocation or avocation, we all may build within ourselves and within our lives an "altar-ed" space where we may practice personal devotion.

When Henri came to Atlanta for our last visit, he bought beautiful and colorful flowers at the airport as a gift for the "altar" of our home. These complemented the planter of now-overgrown greenery he had sent in celebration of our wedding. Before he left the next day, he led us in a prayer service on the deck of our house that overlooks a kudzu-covered ravine lined with old, magnificent trees. This deck serves as my own sanctuary for my morning prayers.

I write this on a Sunday morning when I'm supposed to be in church. I'm resistant to going to church these days. My church has policies that I find contrary to the spirit not only of God, but of spirituality. The people in my local congregation are dear people, and they resist these policies. But there's something about the worship experience itself that I now find confining. The Sunday newspaper gives me better opportunities for reflection on life's meaning and awe at the wondrous gift of life itself.

"Churches, mosques and temples which cover so much hypocrisy and humbug and shut the poorest out of them seem but a mockery of God and [God's] worship when one sees the eternally renewed temple of worship under the vast blue canopy inviting everyone of us to real worship, instead of abusing [God's] name by quarreling in the name of religion." The Mahatma, Mohandes K. Gandhi, in 1942 wrote this truth that appears in a Gandhian "rosary" that I read through from time to time in my morning prayers.

Being from the Reformed tradition, I know that churches are as unfinished as our individual lives, and I should seek to forgive them for their incompleteness as I seek to forgive myself and be forgiven for mine. I am reminded that just four months after Henri had led us in prayer on our deck, I was attending Henri's funeral mass in an unfinished cathedral in Richmond Hill, Ontario, a symbolic site sacralized by the mourners, largely those outcast or marginalized by the church but welcomed by Henri.

ᛜ GOD GRANT ME THE VISION TO DISCERN THOSE SANCTUARIES WITHIN MY BUSY LIFE AND DIFFICULT WORLD IN WHICH I REST IN PEACE, RISE IN HOPE, AND RAISE MY EYES IN WONDER AND MY HANDS IN PRAISE.

When we have no project to finish,
no friend to visit, no book to read, no television
to watch or no record to play, and when we
are left all alone by ourselves we are brought
so close to the revelation of our basic human
aloneness . . . that we will do anything to get
busy again and continue the game.

Reaching Out, 17

In his presentations, Henri almost buzzed the words "we live busy, busy, busy lives." He explained that if someone asks how we are, we proudly say, "Oh, we're very busy." If we are not occupied, we are "preoccupied, which means filling up a space even before we get there"! "We are so afraid of open spaces and empty places that we occupy them with our minds even before we are there," Henri wrote (*Reaching Out,* 53).

On more than one occasion, Henri pointed out that Jesus himself needed a "lonely place" to pray before dawn in Mark 1:35. He went there the morning after a busy day that included calling the disciples, casting out unclean spirits, healing the sick. The "whole city" of Capernaum had "gathered around the door" of Simon and Andrew's home where he was staying. Jesus escaped before the next day began, because that day, as Simon would explain to him, "Everyone is searching for you" (Mark 1:37).

Many people sought out Henri as well. But it is at least equally true that Henri sought out many people. John Mogabgab, Henri's former assistant at Yale and present editor of the spiritual journal *Weavings,* told me that Henri once came to visit, claiming he wanted no engagements. But upon his arrival, he was surprised that no one had organized anything for him to do. "Usually there's someone who wants to meet with me," he told John rather plaintively.

Henri wrote today's quotation in 1975. But in 1996, the final year of his life, in his journal entry of April 22, he describes coming home after a busy day at 10:30 at night and phoning four separate friends to reflect on time they had recently spent together. This is but an example of his own ongoing busyness revealed in *Sabbatical Journey — The Diary of His Final Year.* Just reading of his many travels, visits, masses, preaching, speaking, reading, and writing leaves the reader exhausted! His "sabbatical" was very busy!

Yet that same year on February 26, he wrote to me and a friend:

> Your letter was a great joy to me! Thanks for telling me about your busy lives. Please slow down a little so that you [can] be more creative! I discover myself during this Sabbatical that I am doing more by doing less. . . .
>
> The many projects you both are involved with are all good and useful, but in the long run they leave you dissatisfied and a little empty. . . .
>
> Well, there are some wise thoughts of a usually over-busy old guy! . . .

No wonder Henri took comfort in the words of the sternly ascetic seventh-century John of the Ladder, "If some are still dominated by their former bad habits, and yet can teach by mere words, let them teach. . . . For perhaps, being put to shame by their own words, they will eventually begin to practice what they teach" (*Reaching Out*, 9).

ᢙ BLESS ME WITH SILENCE, SOLITUDE, SEPARATION—JUST MY SELF AND YOUR SPIRIT, O GOD. TOGETHER WE CAN LIFT THE WORLD IN PRAYER, RATHER THAN MY TRYING TO DO IT BY MYSELF.

Thomas Merton describes compassion
as the purifying desert in which we are
stripped of all our false differences and
enabled to embrace each other as the
children of the same God.

Aging, 114

At the same time, Henri can affirm, quoting psychologist Bernice Neugarten, that "increased differentiation occurs over the life cycle" (*Aging,* 59). This means that the uniqueness of an individual grows more pronounced with age, as does a fine wine. I believe that knowing what sets us apart makes us secure enough to recognize what unites us, thus embracing human diversity.

Henri knew what set him apart. When other little boys were playing with toy guns or cars, Henri played priest, dressed in specially made vestments with a child-size altar. Though the priesthood as a vocation might be what was expected of a son in a Roman Catholic family mid-twentieth century, Henri did not fit the expectations of an ordinary diocesan priest. His yearn for adventure led him to serve as a chaplain for a cruise line, then explore the relationship of psychology and religion at the Menninger Clinic in Kansas. He taught that relationship at Notre Dame, and though called to do the same at Yale Divinity School, his inclination was toward spirituality. He was drawn to serve the poor in Latin America, then the disabled of L'Arche. This was no conventional priest.

So on a visit to Los Angeles, it was not surprising when he urged me to take him after a speaking engagement to the community of West Hollywood that I served through the West Hollywood Presbyterian Church. I took him to Studio One, a disco of the era—mirrored bar, et al. His eyes widened and his arms spread as if to vest himself in the shadowy atmosphere of loud music and dancing bodies around him for a different kind of Eucharist, a celebratory Thanksgiving. "There is such a beat here," he said appreciatively.

We then had a drink at a gay video bar called Revolver. Henri was looking around at the hundred or so men with their eyes glued to video screens throughout the pub, alternating music videos with campy film clips. Incredulous at the minimal interaction among the patrons, he said, "I don't see how anyone can possibly enjoy this!" Now, as I recall the incident, I don't remember ever seeing Henri look at a television screen. I don't even remember if Henri *had* a television at Yale. But if he watched TV, I daresay it would have served as an opportunity to bring fellow viewers into conversation.

Finally, we drove by a hot dog stand infamously known at the time as a drug hangout. When I explained this, Henri said eagerly, "Let's stop!" We parked and walked around the tables and chairs and video games of the partially enclosed structure. Henri's intent gazing at various people made it feel as if we were in a zoo. He saw a wigged out couple and asked if I thought they were on drugs. My verification of his impression elicited more wonder on his part than judgment.

Henri's compassion for people did serve as a "purifying desert" in which his difference, set apart as a priest, did not get in the way of others coming to God's table. As he grew older, he grew more secure in welcoming all of God's children, even his own stranger within.

ɷ **May I welcome the stranger outside and the stranger within to your table, O God.**

That's what a monastery is all about.
In the many little things of everyday life
we can recognize the [spiritual] battle.
It can be as small as a desire for a letter
or a craving for a glass of milk.

The Genesee Diary:
Report from a Trappist Monastery, 54

Henri tells the story of a friend who visited him during the first of two prolonged stays at a Trappist monastery. When he took the friend to the airport for his return, Henri began complaining about those who did not acknowledge gifts he had sent, including this friend, to whom he had sent an expensive book. The friend told Henri that, apparently, he couldn't give without expecting something in return. Henri grew defensive and their conversation mundane. Later he inwardly criticized himself for becoming so petty (*The Genesee Diary,* 137–38).

The reader might wonder at the arrogance of the friend who abdicated responsibility for failing to give thanks for the gift. But Henri rightly looked at the beam in his own eye rather than the splinter in his friend's. That's why he had entered the monastery, to let the simple things of life teach him lessons about himself and his relationship with God and others.

Henri had to return again and again to places that helped "the least of these" tutor him: the poor in Peru, the suffering in war-torn Guatemala and Nicaragua, the disabled members of the L'Arche community, even his materially privileged but spiritually impoverished students of all ages. These served as his monasteries out in the world. "Ministry is contemplation," he wrote. "The paradox of the ministry is that we find the God we want to give in the lives of the people to whom we want to give [God]" (*Creative Ministry*, 63). What "the poor" taught him was the confidence of the sparrow for whom God provides, the beauty of the lily in the field whom God adorns.

As I read the Psalms I am struck by the psalmist's confidence in God's personal care and love. The psalmist may wail and whine but believes God is attentive even to human tantrums. The psalmist—or better, psalmists—cry out from every condition, perspective, and feeling, yet affirm their faith in God. I think of Henri as a modern-day psalmist who, through every life experience, happy or sad, meaningful or confusing, life-giving or life-threatening, expressed his faith in God. Some of us have difficulty with the Psalms because of their uncensored expression of disturbing human feelings, even pronouncing a blessing on those who dash the children of enemies on the rocks (Psalm 137:9). We may feel "above" such a feeling. But if our own children had been dashed on the rocks by our enemies, we might very well feel the same thing.

The same may be true of Henri's writing. Not all readers will identify with his anguish, or a particular feeling or experience, or a specific person or people of whom he writes. But his writings may stretch our compassion, our "suffering with," as Henri used to parse the word, to embrace the world.

Ꮿ MAY I BE THE PSALMIST OF MY OWN LIFE, EXPRESSING MY FAITH IN YOU, O GOD, IN EVERY CONDITION, FROM EVERY PERSPECTIVE, WITHIN EVERY FEELING THROUGHOUT MY DAYS.

Much church discussion focuses on the morality
of human behavior: premarital sex, divorce, homosexuality,
birth control, abortion and so on. . . . But when the moral
life gets all the attention, we are in danger of forgetting the
primacy of the mystical life, which is the life of the heart.

The Road to Daybreak, 47–48

The Road to Daybreak is Henri's journal of the year of explo-
ration with the L'Arche (the Ark) international community
founded by French Canadian Jean Vanier in Trosly, France. This
ecumenical community consists of core members with disabilities and their assistants who live together in households.
Henri's reflections begin in late summer and early fall of 1985.

Henri describes in today's text his encounter with Père
Thomas (Father Thomas), the late mystic-in-residence of
L'Arche Trosly. The reader might imagine the successful but
anguished Conway finally meeting Shangri-La's High Lama
in James Hilton's *Lost Horizon.* Like the High Lama of that
idealistic tale, Père Thomas offers spiritual wisdom only a
sage of great age may confer. It is in the context of a multiple-
hour "sermon" spread over two days that Père Thomas offers
the profound insight Henri paraphrases.

The mistaken elevation of moral questions over mystical
questions is one that Jesus confronted time and time again.
Not what goes into a person, but what comes out of a person's heart is what is spiritually important for Jesus. Obeying
the law is helpful, but more important is to love God with all
your heart, mind, and soul, and your neighbor as yourself.

Righteousness is good, but mercy is better. Knowledge of the law is positive, but knowledge of the heart is divine.

Joseph Campbell once said that the mistake of the church in the twentieth century was to reduce Christian faith to morality. Others of us have made the parallel mistake of reducing Christian faith to justice. Churches that focus either on personal morality or social justice to the detriment of cultivating the inner voice of love miss the very inspiration required for both morality and justice. It is when we truly understand ourselves as God's beloved children that we feel called to seek to know and to do what's right. Our status as God's daughters and sons gives us "response-ability."

"Real social action is a way of contemplation, and real contemplation is the core of social action," Henri wrote (*Creative Ministry*, 81). He later wrote

> Life can teach us that although the events of the day are out of our hands, they should never be out of our hearts. . . . When our protests against war, segregation and social injustice do not reach beyond the level of a reaction, then our indignation becomes self-righteous, our hope for a better world degenerates into a desire for quick results, and our generosity is soon exhausted by disappointments. Only when our mind has descended into our heart can we expect a lasting response to well up from our innermost self. (*Reaching Out*, 40)

Henri liked to contrast *react* with *respond*. We are mere reactionaries when we don't allow the events of the day or of our lives to descend into the heart, inspiring a response that springs from a deeper well than our immediate and superficial reactions.

ॐ OPEN MY HEART, GOD. OPEN MY HEART TO RECEIVE ALL I ENCOUNTER TODAY AND HOLD IT THERE.

> The reformer, who is convinced that
> things have to become different, is out
> to convert the world but is tempted at
> the same time to think that he himself
> does not need conversion.

Creative Ministry, 75

Both Thomas Merton and Henri pointed out that, for the Desert Fathers and Mothers who went out into the Egyptian desert in the fourth and fifth centuries to pray, prayer was the place of conversion. Thus prayer is not a way to change God or even others, but a way to allow God to transform us.

I was raised in a Christian milieu that valued the "born-again" experience, a single dramatic conversion. Yet it was a concept I couldn't fathom. I chose to follow Jesus at an early age and was baptized when I was six years old. There was no dramatic change in my life. But ever since, Jesus has changed my life little by little. It has proven true, as Paul wrote the Ephesians, that "God brought [me] to life with Christ" (Ephesians 2:5, NJB). I have experienced some changes that have been more dramatic than others, but even those needed retrospective contemplation to fully comprehend what God was doing in my life.

My first Christian community taught me that prayer was asking for things from God. I found myself frequently asking God to change me in a dramatic way, to make me the way I supposed I was to be. God did change me, but not in the ways I was expecting. I began to relax and determine how God was speaking even through my unchanged parts. I began to rest in God in a world and a church that would not like all of me, that would not let me rest. Little did I know that I was intuitively practicing the prayer of the desert: hesychasm, from the Greek word *hesychia*, which means *to rest*. "My soul is restless, until it rest in thee, O God," as Augustine wrote. The literal translation of the desert father Arsenius's command "to pray always" is "come to rest," as Henri explains *(The Way of the Heart,* 69).

We often pray for God to change others, the world, or our circumstances. As Christians we feel called to convert others or change the world. When I was young, I wanted to convert people. Then I wanted to change the world, converting people in a different way: I became involved in politics, the civil rights movement, the peace movement, other movements seeking justice. Then I decided maybe I could at least change my little part of the world, the church, making it more inclusive, more just. Now, in middle age, I feel blessed if I can change myself!

The Desert Fathers and Mothers viewed prayer not just as a place of conversion for themselves, but for the whole world. As Merton wrote in *The Wisdom of the Desert,* "The Coptic hermits who left the world as though escaping from a [ship]wreck, did not merely intend to save themselves. They knew that they were helpless to do any good for others as long as they floundered about in the wreckage. But once they got a foothold on solid ground, things were different. Then they had not only the power but even the obligation to pull the whole world to safety after them" *(The Wisdom of the Desert,* 23). The "rest" these monastics sought was simply that solid ground, the ability to forget themselves and their own imperfections to better serve (if not save) the world.

ॐ **MAY I REST IN THEE, O GOD, SO I MAY BETTER SERVE OTHERS.**

Gradually, I began to see the
simple fact that those I feared had
great power over me.

Lifesigns, 16

Lifesigns: Intimacy, Fecundity, and Ecstasy in Christian Perspective
describes our need to move from the house of fear to the
house of love, from the world's house to God's house. The
world has power over us when we are afraid of ourselves, of
others, of life itself. In my view, religion becomes a worldly expression of spirituality when it, too, exercises power over us by
making us afraid of ourselves, others, and life. Then it makes
God's house "a den of robbers," robbing our life from us,
rather than a "house of prayer" for all peoples (Mark 11:17),
giving us our lives.

"Fear engenders fear. Fear never gives birth to love,"
Henri writes (*Lifesigns,* 18). I believe the god of fear is a
worldly god, thus an idol. It is the god that commands moral
perfection rather than compassion, vengeance rather than
justice, violence rather than vulnerability, fortresses rather
than communities, closed rather than open communions.
The god of fear is antichrist, because the God of Christ is
love, which "casts out all fear" (see 1 John 4).

Henri uses the Gospel of John and the epistles of John
to talk about God's house of love. He writes of the "first
love": "We love because [God] first loved us (1 John 4:19)."
The epistle leads us into this conclusion by explaining,
"There is no fear in love, but perfect love casts out fear; for

fear has to do with punishment, and whoever fears has not reached perfection in love" (1 John 4:18).

The reason people or things or a worldly god have power over us is because we are afraid of them. What will people think? What if I don't have everything I need (or want)? What if I lose something (or everything)? What if I make God angry? What if God abandons me?

"I will never forget you, I will never forsake you," goes one of the many "little songs" that Henri would call for groups to sing at appropriate times in his presentations. The Gospel of John asserts in its very first chapter that Christ came that we might all be given "power to become children of God, who were born not of blood or of the will of the flesh or of the will of [human beings], but of God" (John 1:12–13). Like the Beloved Son, we, the Beloved Children, do not have our power taken away from us but have it given to us. As beloved children, we do not have to fear abandonment or forsakenness, because even in the absence of feeling God's presence, our relationship with God does not change.

Over and over again the gospel stories tell us not to be afraid: Gabriel said it to Mary, the angels to the shepherds, Jesus to his disciples on several occasions, the angels to the women at the empty tomb. "Perfect love casts out fear." And being in the presence of God is being in the presence of perfect love: "It is I, do not be afraid" (Matthew 14:27).

Even the biblical injunction to "fear the Lord" should not be understood as a psychological description of our relationship with God, as I once heard Brother Thomas Keating point out. Rather it's an appropriate attitude of awe and reverence with which we approach the almighty Creator of the universe.

∾ I AM ALWAYS YOUR CHILD, BELOVED CHILD OF A BELOVED GOD. NOTHING CAN SEPARATE US. AWESOME!

Without the sincere interest, the critical
response and the original contributions of
many students, I would never have been able
to distinguish between what is personal and
what is private, between what is universal
and what is "just me."

Reaching Out, "Acknowledgments"

Though Henri believed that what is personal is most universal, he discretely sensed, often with the help of others, what was "too much information" long before the phrase became a way of signaling a speaker that unwanted details are being provided.

Writers do not work in a vacuum. Henri especially sought out knowledgeable and critical friends to review his manuscripts. Editors advise on content and organization, often with the help of their own readers. Copyeditors look at spelling, grammar, and syntax. Even marketing people sometimes have input in terms of a book's organization, title, and subtitle. And, of course, publishers decide whether to publish at all.

But a nonfiction writer needs more than that. If a book is purportedly about "reality," authors need feedback from as many sources as possible to confirm or confront their notion of what reality is. Henri listened carefully to responses to lectures and sermons, reshaping his material for publications. Henri told me that he also frequently published portions of an upcoming book in magazines, journals, and other periodicals, both to acquire input and to gain interest in a forthcoming book.

The writer's life may serve as metaphor of the spiritual life. If people cultivate the spiritual life in a vacuum, they may mislead themselves and others. Without a good editor—a spiritual director, a spiritual community—such spirituality may become narcissistic, idiosyncratic, even destructive. Without feedback, one can get lost in a spiritual wilderness, fixating on survivalist manna and water or a self-serving oasis rather than moving toward the Promised Land. Without tradition, one is forced to freelance one's spirituality, wasting valuable time and energy reinventing the wheel, so to speak, rather than riding it to a new vista of understanding.

Distrust and cynicism about spiritual leaders and traditions prompt this individualistic approach. Yet that distrust and cynicism are also distrust and cynicism about ourselves. We have been misled, even spiritually abused before. We are not certain of our own spiritual discernment. Marjorie Thompson, a fellow student of Henri and a spiritual director, once said to me that this is the most needed gift in our time, discerning the spirits.

Such discernment may or may not lead us to return to our spiritual roots. Michael Ford observed in his biography *Wounded Prophet* that Henri "came to realize that religious expression is more about a group of people searching for God's love in the ordinary events of life and death in their neighborhoods, rather than in the rituals of institutions or churches" (*Wounded Prophet,* 129). Religion is not what you do with your solitariness, as process theologian Alfred North Whitehead once wrote, but what you do with your connectedness, even in solitude. Our spirituality should lead us into reaching out—as Henri's book title suggests—to others, to God, not navel-gazing.

ᐱ **LEAD ME IN DISCERNING SPIRITUAL COMMUNITY—PAST, PRESENT, AND FUTURE. BLESS ME WITH THE GIFT OF DISCERNING THE SPIRITS THAT GUIDE ME ALONG YOUR PATH, O GOD.**

We have to trust that our stories
deserve to be told—we may discover
that the better we tell our stories, the
better we will want to live them.

Bread for the Journey, April 28

Jan Risse appeared on Henri's doorstep one day simply to bring greetings from L'Arche founder Jean Vanier. Certain she was going to ask him to do something, he kept asking what she wanted. Finally she invited herself in. She stayed in his home while he was away for the day. When he returned, she had prepared an elaborate table for his dinner. He asked where she found the linens, plates, silverware, and candle. She replied that she had found them in his own cupboards.

Of course this is a wonderful metaphor of how unaware we may be of what we have stashed in our own spiritual cupboards. I use it for retreats on spiritual autobiographical writing to illustrate that we have many stories packed away in memory that have shaped our souls. Someone else may show us our treasures by inviting conversation over a pleasant meal. But sometimes we can simply be attentive to our own stories and find the elements to set our own table.

Yet could Henri himself be so unaware, one who at the time of meeting Risse, had already rummaged through his spiritual cupboards to assemble twenty books on spiritual life and ministry? I can't imagine Henri being disingenuous, though my former Yale professor Jim Dittes described Henri as benignly manipulative (Ford, *Wounded Prophet,* 113). But like a child or an artist, Henri could see the same thing as if for the first time. And also like a child or an artist, he had an insecurity that made him doubt he had anything to offer anyone, one that seemed to haunt him his entire life. He was honestly surprised and pleased when people told him how much his writings affected them.

I just came from speaking on a panel to a class of a nursing school. I was introduced as one of two theologians on a panel of three. I used it as a "teaching moment" to say everyone in the room was a theologian, that we all have our words about God (*theo*=God, *logos*=word), but that two of us got paid for it! What may have seemed glib is nonetheless true. Michael Ford points out that Henri reminded students that theologia was first used to describe the highest form of prayer, communion with God. Only since the Enlightenment did it become an academic way of describing God, apart from prayer (*Wounded Prophet*, 107–8).

Many if not most of us have had experiences of communion with God, or intimacy with the sacred. We have a story to tell. In the retreat on spiritual autobiography, I use an idea of Matthew Fox, inviting participants to draw their "spiritual maps," lining out their spiritual paths as creatively as possible, depicting chasms they had to cross, walls to climb, dragons to battle. I suggest they draw their future path as well. It's surprising how intriguing the project is, especially for those less verbal. Then participants describe their maps. The visual cues make the stories easier to tell. But the drawing exercise itself returns them to a childlike sense of awe and wonder at their own spiritual passages, and it is a great leveler in which their words about God (theology) are simple rather than difficult and complex.

ℭ I LOVE TO TELL THE STORY—MY STORY, AND YOURS, HOLY GOD!

Maybe we are so full of our own opinions,
ideas and convictions that we have no space left to
listen to the other and learn from him or her. . . .
To care means first of all to empty our own cup and
to allow the other to come close to us.

Out of Solitude, 42

Henri occasionally used Zen stories to illustrate his points. Within the ellipsis of this quote is the story of a university professor who goes to a master teacher to learn Zen. The master pours him a cup of tea. Once full, he continues to pour until the professor objects, saying, "No more will go in!" The master explains that, like this teacup, the professor is full of his own ideas and must empty his cup to receive.

There is a seeming paradox of yesterday's story about discovering how full our spiritual "cupboards" are and today's call for emptying our "cups." On the one hand, we need to know our spiritual stories and hidden resources. On the other hand, we need to open ourselves to the spiritual stories and hidden resources of others.

When I was at Yale, Henri "emptied his cup" by removing his library from the shelves of his office because of a chance remark of a student about his having so many books. Henri realized how intimidating they must have seemed. What could the student offer a person who had read so much?

Years later, when Henri became aware of gender inclusive language, it meant emptying his books of noninclusive language when reprinted—hence the "him or her" in today's quote rather than the original version's "him."

Yet "when we want to be really hospitable we not only have to receive strangers but also to confront them by an unambiguous presence, not hiding ourselves behind neutrality but showing our ideas, opinions and life style clearly and distinctly. . . . Space can only be a welcoming space when there are clear boundaries" (*Reaching Out*, 70, 69). In other words, we hold within our cupboards an empty cup that may hold another's story. The curvature of the cup are the boundaries we provide within which another may fill our cup.

Recently, during a retreat, a participant offered to bring me a cup of coffee. I watched as he filled a cup with hot water, and I started to object, thinking he misunderstood and was going to offer me tea. Someone else at the table realized my confusion and clarified the situation by commenting how thoughtful he was being, warming my cup.

I believe we can warm our cups to receive a guest's story by following a practice of many Native Americans. When they meet, they first talk about how they're related—their tribal connections. Hearing this, I immediately thought this an excellent metaphor for our most difficult meetings, from debates over controversial issues in the church to summit conferences between nations—discovering first how we're related. Knowing how we belong to one another enables true dialogue of subject with subject.

Ꮗ I EMPTY MY CUP TO RECEIVE GOD. I EMPTY MY CUP TO RECEIVE MY NEIGHBOR. I WARM MY CUP TO RECEIVE THEM WARMLY.

When we think about the people
who have given us hope and have increased
the strength of our soul, we might discover that
they were not the advice givers, warners or
moralists, but the few who were able to articulate in words and actions the human condition
in which we participate and who encourage
us to face the realities of life.

Reaching Out, 43

An old joke goes that two married women were discussing their celibate priest's homily on marriage. "I wish I knew as little about marriage as he does," one quipped.

Daniel Helminiak, a friend, author, and former Catholic priest, has pointed out that when it comes to controversial issues, there is a myth that "the less one knows about a subject, the more reliable one's opinion about it is." In other words, the individual with no vested interest can be objective. By this reasoning, he illustrates, only unmarried people should write about marriage!

We live in an era of support groups in which we seek stories and encouragement from others who share our experience. We seek out therapists who have built-in empathy for what we are going through.

Henri's writings touch readers most deeply when he writes out of his own experience. His lifelong struggle with loneliness became *Out of Solitude* and *Reaching Out.* His woundedness became *The Wounded Healer* and *Cry for Mercy.* His grief over his mother's death became *A Letter of Consolation,* written to his father, and *In Memoriam*. His brush with death became *Beyond the Mirror* and the experience of another's dying became *Our Greatest Gift*. And, as a final example of many, his experience of unrequited love became *The Inner Voice of Love*. Almost all of Henri's books grew out of personal experience, which is why the homilist at his funeral received a tender laugh from us by saying that this was one life experience Henri wouldn't get to write about!

The reason Henri's books did not fall into the popular "all about me" genre of literature current these days is because he always saw his pain, suffering, anguish, faith, joy, and love as part of the larger picture, part of the human experience in which we all participate, part of the human experience in which God's own self participated in Jesus. It was a "living reminder" of the worldwide human adventure.

So we should not be afraid or ashamed to speak or write or pray from our own personal experience, keeping ourselves aware that our experience is but a particular expression of the common human condition. We may serve others by giving them hope and strength for their lives. And we will encourage their discovery of their own experience as a sacred text that God is writing within their souls.

℘ HELP ME TO OFFER MY OWN JOYS AND SORROWS AS GUIDEPOSTS
FOR OTHERS FOLLOWING THE PATH TO YOU, **O GOD**.

All I want to say to you is, "You are
the beloved," and all I hope is that you can
hear these words as spoken to you with all the
tenderness and force that love can hold. My
only desire is to make these words reverberate
in every corner of your being.

Life of the Beloved, 26

Martin Luther called John 3:16 the gospel in miniature: "For God so loved the world . . . " Henri Nouwen's "gospel" could be summed up in "You are the beloved." These were the words Jesus heard at his baptism. These are the words we should have heard at ours. Instead we heard theology: "In the name of the Father, the Son, and the Holy Spirit," unintelligible to those of us baptized as infants, perhaps unclear to those of us baptized as children or adolescents, only a little better understood as adults. Theology does not matter if we have not grasped that we are the Beloved. "And if I have prophetic powers, and understand all mysteries and all knowledge, and if I have all faith, so as to remove mountains, but do not have love, I am nothing" (1 Corinthians 13:2).

In his workshop series, "Healing the Shame that Binds You," John Bradshaw leads participants in an exercise wherein a small group encircles another participant and offers affirmations the person should have heard when born, like: "Welcome to the universe." "I'm so glad you're a boy!" or "I'm so glad you're a girl." And so on. When I witnessed how moving this was, I adapted the idea for a spiritual exercise using biblical affirmations, including, "You are my beloved son/daughter, with whom I am well pleased." (For the full list, see chapter seven of my book, *Coming Out as Sacrament.*) For seminars on Henri Nouwen, I have modified the exercise once more, using affirmations from his writings. Today's quote is the first in the collection. Whichever exercise I employ, participants usually find it deeply moving. They are affected, they say, because they seldom hear such good words spoken to them so plentifully, such positive reassurance offered them. It is both a humbling and expansive experience, humbling because participants want to live up to their high calling as God's beloved, expansive because they feel empowered to do so.

Why do we save our "eulogies" (*eu*=good; *logos*=word), our good words, for funerals and memorial services? Why not *begin* life with positive words? Baptism should have less to do with original sin and more to do with original blessing, reminding us that we are Beloved, that we are God's beloved children, that we are our spiritual community's beloved children.

And why not cheer one another on with good words throughout life? The business manual *The One Minute Manager* challenges employers to catch employees doing something right, affirming them, rather than to catch them doing something wrong. Spiritually this works as well. It encourages us to do the right thing. A few pages later in *Life of the Beloved*, Henri wrote, "From the moment we claim the truth of being the Beloved, we are faced with the call to become who we are. Becoming the Beloved is the great spiritual journey we have to make" (*Life of the Beloved*, 37).

❧ I BASK IN YOUR LOVE FOR ME, O GOD, IMMERSED ONCE MORE IN THE REFRESHING WATERS OF YOUR LOVE, LIFTED INTO THE WARMTH OF YOUR SUN BY YOUR TRUSTWORTHY ARMS.

> "How to live for the glory of God
> and not for your own glory?" . . . The
> first thing to realize is that you are the
> glory of God. . . . "Take this as your
> koan: 'I am the glory of God.'"

The Genesee Diary, 53

In Eastern spirituality, a koan is a word given students at each level of their growth for contemplation, intended to lead to greater awareness. The word may puzzle the student's mind and therefore must be taken to heart. The advice about taking "I am the glory of God" as his koan came from Henri's longtime spiritual director, John Eudes Bamberger, during Henri's stay at the Trappist monastery in upstate New York.

Henri quotes the Russian mystic Theophan the Recluse: "To pray is to descend with the mind into the heart, and there to stand before the face of the Lord, ever-present, all-seeing, within you" (*The Way of the Heart,* 76). One way to descend from mind to heart for the desert mystics was by continuously repeating short prayers, such as "Jesus Christ, have mercy on me." Using "I am the glory of God" as a short prayer, a kind of mantra, enables the thought to descend from the mind to the heart, where it can be embraced and lived.

Yet the thought must start in the mind, so some explanation is necessary. We are made in the image of God, thus *reflecting* God's glory. We are made, *period, revealing* God's glory. Our world has come to exist, with all of its creatures, through a glorious process that, for people of faith, has been divinely inspired and infused with God's glory. "All the world is charged with the grandeur of God," as poet priest Gerard Manley Hopkins observed. We receive God in our hearts or come to know the God of our hearts, depending on our spiritual bent, and that Shekinah (Hebrew root "to dwell" translated as God's presence), or divine glory, may be discerned as we descend from the reservations of the mind to the ruminations of the heart.

The irony is that, as we discover ourselves to be the glory of God, we recognize the glory of God in others. In *Reaching Out*, Henri quotes Thomas Merton's recognition: "There is no way of telling people that they are walking around shining like the sun" (*Reaching Out*, 29). For Merton it is the comprehension that we all belong to God, that division and autonomy alike are illusions, that "it is a glorious destiny to be a member of the human race, though it is a race dedicated to many absurdities and one which makes many terrible mistakes: yet, with all that, God Himself gloried in becoming a member of the human race!" (Thomas Merton, *Conjectures of a Guilty Bystander* [New York: Doubleday, 1968], 157–58). Merton compares his enlightenment to having the winning ticket in a cosmic lottery.

So affirming "I am the glory of God" is not "all about me" but all about us. It is the divine life in which we all participate, as process philosopher Charles Hartshorne depicted it. "For in [God] we live and move and have our being," the apostle Paul quotes a Greek poet in Acts 17:38. If only we could fully embrace the reality of our existence, we could fully embrace one another.

ᴐᴠ I AM THE GLORY OF GOD! YOU ARE THE GLORY OF GOD! THANKS BE TO GOD!

A desire for communion has been
part of you since you were born. The pain
of separation, which you experienced as a
child and continue to experience now,
reveals to you this deep hunger.

The Inner Voice of Love, 95

During the relatively intimate graveside service that followed
Henri's funeral mass, a member of his family told of Henri in
his crib always reaching out his arms to be picked up. Henri
had told me the same story, but explained further that the
baby experts of that time advised new parents against cod-
dling. So his pleas and cries were ignored, and he felt it had
left a very deep wound in him. Henri connected this personal
pain to that of the human condition. His early "reaching out"
renders the title *Reaching Out* more poignant for the book he
once called closest to his own Christian experience.

Notions about God, like notions about child rearing,
change. The Bible tells the story of that change, a sweeping
epic from a magnificent, all-powerful God creating the universe to a liberating deity befriending an oppressed people to
an all-vulnerable baby reaching out his arms to be picked up
from a manger in Bethlehem. His pleas and cries for communion were ignored by the dominant culture, and he was
wounded. In doing so, Jesus gave us the sacrament of Communion and the communion of saints, the church—both a
foretaste of God's commonwealth in which God "will wipe
every tear from [our] eyes. Death will be no more; mourning
and crying and pain will be no more." (Revelation 21:4).

Henri first "played" Communion when he was eight years
old (*Can You Drink the Cup?* 14). Once he was ordained, he

celebrated the Eucharist almost every day of his priesthood, so vital it was for him. Throughout his nearly forty years of ministry, notions of the sacrament changed in the church and in him. His first mass on July 22, 1957, the day after his ordination, he faced an altar with his back to the congregation, holding a bejewelled golden chalice his Uncle Anton, a priest, had given him. Only the priest drank from the cup in those days. By the end of his life, he celebrated Communion facing the congregation gathered around a low-lying table on which sat clear glass chalices holding wine for all to see and all to drink. In *Can You Drink the Cup?* Henri uses the contrast to demonstrate how his ministry and his celebration of Communion had changed.

Daybreak, the L'Arche community in Toronto that he served, welcomes Catholics and Protestants, and Henri's celebration of the Eucharist welcomed all Christians. His funeral mass welcomed not only Christians, but people of other faiths or no faith. So that no one felt excluded, there was no announcement of "Catholics only" when it came time for the distribution of the gifts. Blessings were given to individuals who chose not to receive Communion, and prayers were offered that the Body of Christ might be one once more. Even arrangements at the Catholic cemetery were made according to Henri's desire to be buried alongside members of his community, both Protestant and Catholic. In death as in life, Henri's spirit was reaching out to overcome "the pain of separation" that the Body of Christ still suffers.

I believe the desire for communion is central to the spiritual life. Maybe that's why the quest for the Holy Grail— supposedly the chalice Jesus used—captured the laity's imagination in medieval times and still today. We hunger to break the bread of Christ together and share the wine that restores our souls.

☙ BREAD OF HEAVEN: BY FEEDING US, UNITE US. CUP OF SALVATION: BY GIVING US DRINK, HELP US BECOME ONE.

When we live with a solitude of heart,
we can listen with attention to the words and
worlds of others, but when we are driven by
loneliness, we tend to select just those remarks
and events that bring immediate satisfaction
to our own craving needs.

Reaching Out, 26

Loneliness is a gnawing hunger, while solitude is to have one's hunger satisfied without being stuffed. The more hungry we are, the less particular we may be about what we eat. The more lonely we are, the less particular we may be about how we connect with others. And, just as starving makes people desperate, so loneliness brings out our desperation. In either scenario, we may act out of our anxiety, seeking a quick fix to our hunger or our loneliness. This may prompt us to exploit or manipulate others, or allow ourselves to be exploited or manipulated.

No matter what a televangelist or a pop guru might tell you, the spiritual life is not a quick fix or drive-through. Conversion experiences may happen along our spiritual paths, but they need follow-through. At a store in Washington, D.C., I was signing copies of my last book, *Reformation of the Heart,* meditations for the Christian seasons of Advent, Epiphany, and Lent. A young man from a charismatic Christian background stopped by to tell me how much one of my earlier books had meant to him. But I noticed he wasn't buying the new book, and I asked him why, wondering if it was a financial problem. He explained that his background did not include observing the Christian calendar. I replied that my religious background didn't either, but that I had found it a helpful discipline for remembering the Christian story.

His reply surprised me a little, "Ah, there's that word," he said.

"What word?" I asked.

"Discipline."

Spiritual abuse in his religious upbringing made him associate "discipline" with punishment. In addition, his denomination had taught him that "true" spirituality had to be spontaneous, serendipitous, dramatic, and emotional. After all, Jesus himself said, "The wind blows where it chooses, and you hear the sound of it, but you do not know where it comes from or where it goes. So it is with everyone who is born of the Spirit" (John 3:7–8). The idea that spirituality might be a discipline to cultivate was foreign to him.

Henri's quest and his corpus were all about developing a spiritual discipline to pursue a life in the Spirit that would serve as a foundation for ministry. The Spirit may blow where it will, but one has to place oneself in a position to receive it, just as one has to open a window or go outside to feel the breeze. Or, said another way, Saul would never have had the transforming conversion experience he had on the road to Damascus had he not been on the road in the first place. Thus we must find our spiritual paths and walk them.

The solitude of which Henri wrote is the spiritual path along which "we can listen with attention to the words and worlds of others."

֎ O GOD, HELP ME CARVE OUT OF EACH DAY'S AGENDA A SANCTUARY IN WHICH TO OPEN MY HANDS, MY HEART, AND MY MIND TO YOUR WORD AND WORLD AND THE WORD AND WORLDS OF OTHERS.

Hospitality is not a subtle invitation to adopt
the life style of the host, but the gift of a chance
for the guest to find his or her own.

Reaching Out, 51

Henri contrasted hostility and hospitality. The root word of hostility is *hostis: stranger, enemy.* The root word of hospitality is *hospes: host, guest.* Hospitality "means primarily the creation of a free space where the stranger can enter and become a friend instead of an enemy" (*Reaching Out,* 51). Receiving strangers as welcome guests without an agenda is a manifestation of a mature spirituality. An Episcopal guest house I frequented once awakened guests in time for matins, early morning prayers. Then the brothers of the order realized this contradicted their intent of hospitality. What had initially been viewed as an invitation for guests to participate in the life of the community seemed now like "a subtle invitation to adopt the life style of the host."

In the harsh environments that spawned the Jewish, Christian, and Muslim religions, hospitality was not simply a courtesy but a moral obligation. Water, food, and shelter were hard to come by in the wilderness. According to Jewish scripture, the whole city of Sodom was destroyed because of its inhospitality to strangers (Genesis 19). Yet when those same strangers previously were welcomed by Abraham and Sarah (Genesis 18), they were able to reveal the promise of a child that would be born to them, fulfilling God's covenant that the couple would give rise to a great nation. Henri uses this as metaphor to suggest that welcoming guests allows them to reveal their promise, because as guests, "We will never believe that we have anything to give unless there is someone who is able to receive" (*Reaching Out*, 61).

I once worked alongside a pastor who, though a very good and able man, was very protective of his private life, and not so welcoming of the struggles of others. I was of a different bent, and tended to speak openly about my personal challenges and questions—hopefully, not overwhelming people, but letting them know I did not claim to "have it all together." I found that many church members sought me for pastoral counseling, viewing me as someone who was able to hear their questions because they knew I didn't have all the answers.

Pastors and spiritual guides and teachers will often say they learn as much from the people with whom they work as they teach. Spirituality requires community, a safe house, a sanctuary in which we are at the same time guests and hosts. When I took a campus ministry internship in Philadelphia, Henri suggested I retreat at nearby Pendle Hill, a Quaker retreat center where students are teachers and teachers are students. This is the nature of spiritual community.

Every time and place was an opportunity for Henri's hospitality, welcomed or not. I remember a particularly harrowing drive after he picked me up from the Toronto airport in which Henri was far more interested in what had been happening to me than what was happening on the road! Henri, who normally sped—as he was always a little behind—was driving so slowly cars were whizzing past us, and he seemed oblivious to their impatience.

What might not be the safest thing to do in traffic seems like the sanest thing to do in these fast-paced, impatient times.

ᐷ THANK YOU, GOD, THAT I DON'T HAVE IT ALL TOGETHER. THANK YOU FOR THE QUESTIONS, THE DOUBTS, THE STRUGGLES. MAY THEY BE THE BUILDING BLOCKS OF A SAFE HOUSE FOR THE QUESTIONS, THE DOUBTS, THE STRUGGLES OF OTHERS.

The most subtle desire for power, and
the most difficult to overcome is the desire for thanks.

Creative Ministry, 74

Every morning when I say the prayer that Jesus taught his disciples, I alternate among "trespasses" and "debts" and "sins." When I pray "Forgive us our debts as we forgive our debtors," I often think of my need to release people whom I think "owe me" for what I have done for them, either collectively or individually. It seems a small thing to do in the broader context of asking God to forgive us our debts—after all, we owe God everything!

But it is a difficult concept to live. In a culture and even a church in which people feel entitled, we feel people owe us much we haven't earned. Some of us enjoy "privilege" because we are part of dominant segments of society (class, race, gender, sexual orientation, etc.) or of the church (hierarchy, clergy, lay leaders, etc.). Others of us feel the world owes us because we are underprivileged as marginalized people. And we live in a litigious culture and a litigious church, in which we sue in civil courts or force to ecclesiastical proceedings those whom we believe have wronged us or owe us something. Perhaps we should add to the controversy of those who want the Ten Commandments emblazoned on the walls of criminal courts by suggesting we have writ large over civil courts the words, "Forgive us our debts, as we forgive our debtors."

Yet even in our misguided sense that others "owe" us something, we reflect our own indebtedness—that is, that we all often fail to adequately give thanks. And in failing to give thanks, we miss "the spiral of thanksgiving" that Brother David Stendl-Rast spoke of in one of my classes with Henri. He used the illustration of a baby who cries, and his mother offers him a rattle to play with. The baby smiles in thankful pleasure, and the mother, touched by his response, sweeps him up in her arms, lifting him and herself to a higher level of ecstasy.

That's what happens when we make a point of giving thanks. A phone call, a thank-you card, a face-to-face "thank you," raises the gift, the receiver, and the giver to a higher level of joy. This also happens in giving thanks to God. It lifts us to the heart of the Giver of all things good and beautiful.

But think of the shame or the bad feelings generated by a demand for thanks! Then it becomes less than a free gift, a free response of a free will. Then it truly feels like we "owe" someone something, that it was not a gift at all but an expectation of a certain response, a way of exercising the giver's power over the receiver. Better for the giver to feel good in the giving, remembering Jesus' words, "It is more blessed to give than to receive" (Acts 20:35). And if we go unthanked, better that we remember our own gifts from other people and from God that have gone unthanked.

And yet, still better for the receiver to acknowledge the gift, giving thanks. That is the heart of spiritual worship when it comes to thanking God. Worship comes from root words meaning "to create worth," and what offers a sense of worth and value more than giving without expectation and receiving with thanks?

༄ FORGIVE US OUR DEBTS, AS WE FORGIVE OUR DEBTORS.

> You are still afraid to die. That fear is
> connected with the fear that you are not
> loved. Your question "Do you love me?"
> and your question "Do I have to die?"
> are deeply connected.

The Inner Voice of Love, 91

The resurrected Jesus asked Peter three times, "Do you love me more than these?" (John 21:15–19). Peter's threefold assurance is Gospel writer John's way of balancing out Peter's threefold denial of the arrested Jesus (John 18:15–18, 25–27).

During the period Henri wrote the journal that became *The Inner Voice of Love,* he was grieving the rejection by someone who essentially said "no" to Henri's unarticulated question, "Do you love me more than these?" It was described as "an interrupted friendship," but it was more than that. It was the dashing of his dreams of having a "significant other." Shattered as he was, Henri's community sympathetically suggested he go somewhere for healing, nurture, counseling, and spiritual direction. From that place Henri phoned me several times. I don't remember the specifics of our conversations, but I remember the angst in his voice. I imagined a bleak, wintry horizon with low-hanging clouds, no doubt a reflection of Henri's depression.

Just months before, we had had a conversation about celibacy in a Toronto-area diner. Henri told me he believed in his vocation as a celibate priest, yet he wistfully missed a companion in life. For those with eyes to see and hearts to recognize it within Henri's writings, Jesus seemed sometimes to serve as a substitute for this absent partner, and his enthusiasm meeting new friends as recorded in journals, revealed his undying hope to meet that special someone.

Henri spoke to me of the death of his Uncle Anton, a priest who had passed on his ordination chalice to Henri. People grieved, he told me, but then left the graveside to socialize, and their lives resumed, little changed. He said that when he died, he yearned to have one person whose life would be radically altered by his passing.

One of the liabilities of our faith affirmation that God's "love is stronger than death" (the essence of Song of Solomon 8:6–7) is that we mistakenly conclude that we can postpone love. When we view our lives as eternal, then the opportunities of giving and receiving love seem endless. We can miss time with our children, visits with our parents, and evenings with our spouses because what we miss in this life we can catch up on in the next. We can give up a personal life to fulfill our vocations, a personal relationship to serve our communities, essentially what celibacy calls its practitioners to do.

We all have "practiced celibacy" more or less in pursuit of other goals. When we have done so out of love for a greater good, that could be viewed as noble. But when we have done so out of fear of intimacy or a belief that we will not die, or when it has been imposed on us, it could be viewed as unhealthy.

Jesus called us to love more than live. Love God, love neighbor, love enemies—yet "greater love has no one" than offering one's life for one's friends. Love is eternal even when life is not. As Henri wrote to me and my partner, "A life of contemplation, creative writing, and great attentiveness to each other's needs gives you three ways of catching the eternal already now. What comes from the center of your heart *stays*, because it belongs to God" (private correspondence, February 26, 1996).

ॐ **HELP US CATCH THE ETERNAL NOW!**

> The presence of Christ in the Eucharist
> becomes a "special problem" only when
> we have lost our sense of His presence
> in all that is, grows, lives, and dies.
>
> *Creative Ministry,* 103

The Eucharist or Holy Communion is a taste of God. *How* God is present in the bread and wine of this central Christian sacrament is less important than *that* God is present. Belief is needed to fully embrace the presence of God in any sacrament, official or informal.

Many who read this have shared my despair that we Christians spend so much time bickering over how to celebrate the Eucharist, what it means, who is and who is not included at the table. If Jesus were only here to offend our Eucharistic sensibilities by welcoming the woman of ill repute to Simon the leper's table, inviting himself to tax collector Zaccheus's house, dining with religious outcasts, feeding the thousands of poor who were also hungry for his message! Jesus had a way of "mixing things up" that offended those who tried to neatly order the spirituality of his time and is just as offensive to those who enforce religious purity in our time.

Henri tells the poignant story of visiting Daybreak core member Trevor in a mental hospital (*Can You Drink the Cup?* 63–66). The hospital administration had invited Henri to meet staff and other invited guests for lunch in the Golden Room, but to Henri's dismay, Trevor could not be included because patients were not admitted. At Henri's insistence, an exception was made and Trevor was invited. As lunch was underway, Trevor stood and invited all to lift their glasses in a toast, making the hospital administrators apprehensive. Then he led them in a song, "When you're happy and you know it, lift your glass!" Trevor thus transformed a somewhat formal gathering into a happy family. Who proved the healer in this room full of healers?!

This should ultimately be the meaning of the Eucharist: a meal that mixes things up by including everyone at the table, regardless of class, ability, education, sexuality, gender, piety, race, nationality, and so on. But also a meal that reminds us that every meal is sacred, that every thing reveals God's presence.

These days I skim the religion section of the paper, because I rarely meet God there, and carefully read the science section, where the God of creation comes alive for me in the discovery of the extensive cosmos, the wondrous diversity of creatures, the amazing complexity of the body. When I see God in all that lives, moves, and breathes, I remember that we do not make God present in a particular ritual or sacrament by specific ways of practicing it or receiving it. God is already present, and the sacrament is only a pathway to recognizing it.

That's why I believe that an "invocation" should never be thought to invoke God's presence, but rather to invoke our own mindfulness that God is already here.

ᔕ **WHEN YOU SEE GOD AND YOU KNOW IT, STRIKE A SMILE!**

In being present to him I was hearing an inner
voice of love beyond all the activities of care.

Adam, 53

Out of context, one could imagine the "him" referring to God
or a lover. Instead it is applied to Adam, the core member
whom Henri assisted: bathing, dressing, and breakfasting
him through his morning routine. Adam could not speak,
though he did find other ways to communicate a little, and
he could not get around on his own.

A pastoral theologian and minister visited Henri and
Adam, and harshly questioned Henri's "wasting" his time with
disabled people who could not understand him, when he could
be doing so much good inspiring students. Shocked, Henri did
not respond to his friend. But in writing about the episode,
Henri explains in this book, published posthumously, how his
mornings with Adam had been "transforming" for him.

Was Henri projecting onto the *tabula rasa* of Adam whatever insights Henri himself achieved? Was Adam meeting
Henri's needs for an intimate relationship that he could not
have, because his celibacy denied him "particular friend-
ships" as well as having his own children? Possibly.

(I want to be clear that I am not implying any inappro-
priate relationship. Also, Adam was in his thirties, but young
enough to be Henri's son.)

But what is clearer still is that Adam served as a kind of
inscrutable Zen master who communicated little and yet led
his student to his own enlightenment. Adam could also be re-
garded as the ultimate Rogerian, engaging in the purest form
of client-centered therapy. Because Henri learned things

about himself from Adam that no book and no teacher could teach him, not even the Bible. Jean Vanier, the founder of L'Arche, had taught him that L'Arche was "not built around the word but around the body" (*Adam*, 46). Being entrusted with Adam's body, Henri found, "was bringing me closer to myself and to my own body" (*Adam*, 49). Henri learned he not only *had* a body, but he *was* his body, telling himself, "Don't let your words become separated from your flesh" (*Adam*, 49).

Anyone who knew Henri could give you a funny anecdote about how disconnected Henri seemed from his body, like the time at dinner, when another dinner companion and I were concerned that Henri's sleeve was going to wipe the butter dish clean as he kept motioning in conversation!

And anyone ministering to another, whether as a professional or a volunteer, family member or friend, might describe a similar experience of hearing an inner voice of love in the process of serving another. I sometimes lead people in a memory exercise of returning to a moment when they felt God smiling on their lives, and though there are the usual share of glorious moments, watching a sunset or sitting beside a still pond, there are also "uglier" moments, holding the hand of a dying friend or changing a baby's diaper, when individuals heard God saying to them, "You are my beloved, with whom I am well pleased."

Meditation and daily prayer are not the only nor always the best ways to hear that inner voice of love. We hear it as we perform acts of charity or challenge injustice. We hear it when we tell the truth to empower the vulnerable or bite our tongues to spare someone's feelings. We hear it when we welcome a stranger like Adam into our lives or the stranger within into our awareness.

∞ KEEP ME ATTENTIVE TO THE TEACHERS IN MY LIFE DISGUISED AS STRANGERS, PARISHIONERS, CLIENTS, PATIENTS, NEIGHBORS, OUTSIDERS, OPPONENTS, AND EVEN MYSELF.

I might not get a statue,
or even a memorial plaque, but I am
constantly concerned that I not be forgotten, that somehow I will live on in
the thoughts and deeds of others.

The Return of the Prodigal Son, 119

Move over, Henri. As pure as our motives might be, all of us on a spiritual quest are not doing this just for God or the greater good. We want to make a difference. "Our" difference.

Henri writes of this in *The Return of the Prodigal Son* as his desire for power, wanting his advice followed, his help thanked, his money used his way, his good deeds remembered. He told me of having dinner at some charity to which he contributed and being disturbed to find the extravagance of each place setting, which included an individual rose in a vase. The executive director pointed out the nonprofit organization's generous hospitality, and Henri had wanted to reply, "You can afford to be generous with someone else's money!"

Nonprofits and religious institutions walk a tightrope between appearing professional and grateful as well as being good stewards of donors' funds. Is the brochure or annual report too slick? Are the offices too nice? Are the salaries too high? The fund-raisers too extravagant? These are appropriate concerns, but they also reflect the strings attached to their contributors' "gifts."

Money is a symbol of all we give. When we counsel someone, we want to see their lives change. When we contribute ideas or time to a group or movement, we want to see the group or movement improve. We also expect appreciation for our efforts, as simple as seeing our name listed with thanks in a church newsletter or as grand as being named "volunteer of the year." We want our "investments" to pay off!

Henri saw this as his desire for control. He uses the metaphor of the forgiving father in Jesus' parable about the prodigal. The father doesn't demand the prodigal repay him his inheritance, either in money or work, or groveling or even gratitude. Henri wanted to be like the father: after all, he was called "Father" Nouwen!

Jesus' parable has been understood as a story about the graciousness of God. But the story, for Henri, is also about spiritual maturity. He had long thought of himself as the prodigal in the story, traveling far from his own family and country pursuing his own goals; subsequently he came to understand himself as the resentful elder brother as well, wishing to be acknowledged for doing the right things, such as becoming a priest. But then he had been challenged by Sue Mosteller in his community, "Henri, we need you to be the father!" After all, that was his role as chaplain of Daybreak, the L'Arche community in Toronto.

"Be perfect . . . as your heavenly Father is perfect," Jesus admonished his disciples (Matthew 5:48). A better translation of the phrase "be perfect" is "be mature." Be mature as your God in heaven is mature, who lets the rain fall and the sun shine on the just and the unjust, those who do God's will as well as those who don't. The God of such magnanimous equity that Jesus preaches is a God of persuasion rather than coercion, a model of vulnerability in Jesus and not a control freak.

And yet few are remembered as well as Jesus, who has lived on in the words and deeds of innumerable others.

ᐯ **HELP ME TO LET GO: OF THE INHERITANCE I DEMAND, OF THE CREDIT I EXPECT, OF THE CONTROL I DESIRE.**

From [my mother] I had come to feel
an unqualified acceptance which had little to
do with my being good or bad, successful or
unsuccessful, close by or far away.

In Memoriam, 34

Henri's look-alike brother Laurent pointed out to biographer Michael Ford that his brother's God was not a demanding one but one who loved us first, concluding, "Henri might have been prepared for that insight by his struggles with a demanding father, but he never perceived God that way" (*Wounded Prophet*, 77). In the margin of that page I wrote, exasperated, "His mother was his model for God!! Not the father!"

In several of his books, Henri's difficult relationship with the somewhat stiff patriarch of the family is discussed openly, most clearly in *A Letter of Consolation* written to his father after the death of Henri's mother, a companion to *In Memoriam* about Henri's own experience of her passing. In *Letter*, Henri confronts many of the issues that have kept them apart. Later he writes of the strict table etiquette his father enforced when he was growing up in *Can You Drink the Cup?* but of a warming relationship in later life in *Our Greatest Gift* and *Sabbatical Journey*.

One could psychologize Henri's relationship with his parents, pointing out that sensitive boys often have a special bond with their mothers, and that fathers frequently put distance from sons that they perceive as unmasculine. But it would be more helpful, I believe, to "theologize" Henri's relationship with his parents: the father represented the patriarchal view of a demanding God the Father in control, and the mother represented a more feminist view of a vulnerable God the Mother with compassion.

Henri did not always do well with feminists, but he was very popular among women generally, as well as sensitive men. It did not surprise me that, when I wrote an op-ed article for the Atlanta paper about Henri after his death, the phone calls I received all came from women. I think Henri's appeal is that, without consciously trying, he was balancing out the patriarchal church he represented with a Mother God. Out of context, if the original pronoun is inserted in today's quote, Henri could be speaking of his view of a Mother God: "From her I had come to feel an unqualified acceptance which had little to do with my being good or bad, successful or unsuccessful, close by or far away."

This is reminiscent of, "You are my beloved, with whom I am well pleased." It is also reminiscent of the forgiving father in the parable of the Prodigal, to which he devoted an entire book based on Rembrandt's painting of that story. Henri pointed out that the father in the painting welcomed and surrounded the prodigal with a masculine hand and a feminine hand.

In the face of the patriarchal religion of his time, Jesus represented at least an androgynous if not a feminine side of God. His ministry included women disciples, such as Mary Magdalene, Joanna, Susanna, and "many others," according to Luke 8:2-3, who provided resources. And the early church benefited from female leaders frequently named in Paul's epistles. Later, before the Reformation gave God a shot of testosterone, more definitively masculinizing God, the church had women in religious vocation writing even of "Mother Jesus."

I believe that when the church errs in its understanding of God, the Spirit sends a correction. In the face of an increasingly rigid and exclusive church, Henri's popularity may be because we need to remember God's motherly, unconditionally inclusive love now more than ever.

∞ GOD, THANK YOU FOR WELCOMING US HOME AND GATHERING US ON YOUR LAP.

When it is true that the image you carry in
your mind can affect your physical, mental, and
emotional life, then it becomes a crucial question
as to which images we expose ourselves or allow
ourselves to be exposed.

Gracias! 31

A friend who is an Episcopal priest in an order that requires chastity told me after returning from service in Quito, Ecuador, that while there, he seldom thought about sex. He realized it was because, unlike in the States, he was not being bombarded by billboard and television images that were constantly reminding him of sexuality.

Henri wrote about this phenomenon in Bolivia, attending language school in preparation for service in Peru. He was reading Jerry Mander's book *Four Reasons for the Elimination of Television.* Its basic premise is that we become what we see. Henri writes, "These imposed images actually make us into the world which they represent, a world of hatred, violence, lust, greed, manipulation, and oppression" (*Gracias!* 31).

At the very least, in my view, these images throw us off center, making us uncertain of our own identity and path, of what's right and wrong, or, more to the point in our peer-driven culture, what's in and what's out.

Henri applies this thinking to prayer, which "also has much to do with imagining" (*Gracias!* 30). How we imagine God affects not only how we pray, but how we view ourselves. Whether we think of God as a demanding father or a compassionate mother, as examples, makes all the difference in how we view our relationship with God and our own identity in that relationship. Henri writes that "Christ came to let us reimagine" that "we are created in the image of God." Reimagining this "leads us to our true identity" (*Gracias!* 31).

Decades after Henri wrote this, reactionary forces in several mainstream Protestant denominations in the United States raised a ruckus about an ecumenical women's gathering whose theme was "Reimagining God." Conservatives disapproved of the questioning of bloody atonement theories, the use of milk and honey in a ritual rather than bread and wine, and the recovery of Sophia (Wisdom) as the feminine side of God. As Joseph Campbell said of interfaith warfare, the reactionary forces were "stuck in their metaphor" of God, failing to understand that their own "God" was not God's true self, but a referent, a metaphor, their own way of "imagining" God. God is way beyond human knowledge, one of the reasons biblical writers insisted that God could only be known through revelation, a revelation of God's identity and of our own that can only be viewed "in a mirror, dimly" (1 Corinthians 13:12).

One of the greatest preachers of the twentieth century, Harry Emerson Fosdick, a Baptist, wrote, "The central trouble in the religious thinking of many people lies here: *the new knowledge of the universe has made their childish thoughts of God inadequate, and instead of getting a worthier and larger idea of God to meet the new need, they give up all vital thought about God whatsoever*" [emphasis Fosdick's] (Fosdick, *The Meaning of Prayer*, 98).

As a contemporary tree of the knowledge of good and evil, the media unveil to us our naked struggle to be like gods, making us ashamed, forgetting who we are. That's why we need prayer, to reimagine walking with God in the cool of the evening as God's first son and daughter did, reminding us of our true identity as God's beloved children, made in our Creator's image.

ल्ल HELP ME REMEMBER "HOW GREAT THOU ART" AND "HOW WONDERFULLY, AWESOMELY MADE I AM."

A true spirituality cannot be
constructed, built, or put together; it has to be
recognized in the daily life of people who search
together to do God's will in the world.

Gracias! 6

The key word for Henri here is "recognized." Those with
eyes to see and ears to hear (favorite spiritual metaphors of
Jesus) may recognize God's kingdom, or commonwealth, in
their midst. In Lima, Peru, Henri was hosted by the Maryknoll Society, whose first objective he quotes: "To recognize
and elaborate a mission of spirituality which integrates community, prayer, a simple life-style, apostolic work, and commitment to the poor." This was a critical reimagining of the
Maryknoll mission, which previously might have been perceived as a kind of "spiritual colonialism." Henri quotes a
Maryknoll priest, Ralph Davila: "It is the change from selling
pearls to hunting for the treasure" (*Gracias!* 7). In other
words, together with the poor they would search "for the
treasure hidden in the ground on which they stand," expressing solidarity (*Gracias!* 8).

The advantage of this fresh understanding of mission was
evident to me on a visit to Nicaragua in 1984, several years
after Henri wrote *Gracias!* Under the organization of Church
World Service, our group of twenty United Methodists, Disciples, and Presbyterians met with, among others, a Roman
Catholic bishop, a diplomat of the American embassy, and a
Maryknoll nun. Of the three, the Maryknoll sister seemed to
be the most in touch with what we had ourselves experienced

among people in the barrios and churches and countryside we visited. The bishop's view was soured by the Roman Catholic hierarchy losing power with the revolution, and the American embassy official gave the party line of an administration that was funding the contras, the counterrevolutionaries. But the Maryknoll sister, who was not in a nice bishop's office or a barricaded, moated embassy, spoke informally with us in a small garden about what she witnessed happening among the people, telling us their stories. My heart sensed she was closer to the people and thus closer to Jesus. Despite her relative powerlessness, she would have been considered "subversive" by the other two. As Henri asked in a similar context, "Can we be true Christians without being considered to be subversives in the eyes of the oppressors?" (*Gracias!* 29).

"Seeing God in the world and making [God] visible to each other is the core of ministry as well as the core of the contemplative life," Henri wrote of his own experience in Latin America (*Gracias!* 20–21). He echoes the apostle Paul's own description of spiritual community: "And all of us, with unveiled faces, seeing the glory of the Lord as though reflected in a mirror, are being transformed into the same image from one degree of glory to another; for this comes from the Lord, the Spirit" (2 Corinthians 3:18).

ᐂ WITH OTHERS, MAY I SEEK TO DO YOUR WILL IN THE WORLD. MAY YOUR SPIRIT IN ME RECOGNIZE YOUR SPIRIT IN OTHERS, BONDING US AS A COMMUNITY TO TRANSFORM YOUR WORLD.

> Every time you feel hurt, offended or
> rejected, you have to dare to say to yourself:
> "These feelings, strong as they may be, are not
> telling me the truth about myself. The truth,
> even though I cannot feel it right now, is that I
> am the Beloved from all eternity and am held
> safe in an everlasting embrace."
>
> *Life of the Beloved,* 49

Henri is writing this to his friend who had asked for a book for spiritual beginners. In regards to feeling hurt, offended, or rejected, Henri was always a spiritual beginner. Often this theme appears in his books, even in the midst of his work with the poor in Peru. As if making a New Year's resolution, Henri there made this Ash Wednesday resolve: "I have slowly become aware of what my Lenten practice might be. It might be the development of some type of 'holy indifference' toward the many small rejections I am subject to. . . . " (*Gracias!* 150).

There's little doubt that Henri's insecurity prompted him to imagine slights. We were to have dinner together when he was visiting Los Angeles one weekend. I had been leading a retreat in Santa Barbara, but my return to L.A. was literally blocked by a railroad car spill next to the highway I was to travel, transforming a two-hour drive into an eight-hour detour. Since I could not have returned in time for dinner, I stayed at the retreat house, to Henri's consternation. My friend George Lynch kept the dinner appointment but said Henri kept questioning why I couldn't be there, as if I were avoiding him. The irony was that he had not planned our dinner in advance, but had called me during the retreat to arrange it on the spur of the moment.

I hesitate telling this story, because it reveals Henri's naked-ness, as it were, his vulnerability. And to some readers, his per-sonal complaints in his books might seem whiny. It's like the discomfort we feel when the psalmist calls for bloody revenge against his enemies. It's not like we haven't been there, whin-ing ourselves or feeling vengeful. But we feel uncomfortable if our spiritual guides confess the same feelings we sometimes entertain. They are supposed to be "above" all that.

Yet it is precisely because Henri was not above all of that that he can guide us in our spiritual quest for the inner voice of love. Doubting others loved him made him seek out the love of God all the more, ferreting out the hidden springs and the unseen manna that our faith provides in the wilder-ness of rejection. The psalmist usually ends fits of despair or woundedness expressing hope in God *anyway*. So did Henri, as he ends his journal entry in *Gracias!* "Maybe all these small rejections are reminders that I am a traveler on the way to a sacred place where God holds me in the palm of [God's] hand" (*Gracias!* 151).

And in his final week of life, Henri was able to let go of these rejections. He told his friend, Nathan Ball, director of Daybreak, to tell people he asked forgiveness of everyone and offered his forgiveness to all. In a sense, it was his "forgive them, for they didn't know what they were doing" as well as "forgive me, because I didn't know what I was doing either."

For Henri, mutual forgiveness was central to community, in life and in death.

∾ HELP ME TO FORGIVE, EVEN AS I HAVE BEEN FORGIVEN, REMEMBERING YOUR STEADFAST LOVE AND GRACIOUS MERCY.

Our inner sanctum, that inner, holy
place, that sacred center in our lives
where only God may enter, that is as
important for our lives as the domes are
for the city of Rome.

Clowning in Rome, 38

For Henri, intimacy is only possible when we have "a deep respect for that holy place within and between us, that space that
should remain untouched by human hands" (*Clowning*, 40).

Think of wanting or having your own room as a child, or
having a secret or private place in which you hid or played—
a tree house, a doll house, a writing desk, a park or stream,
even an imaginary place in your mind. Perhaps you escaped
to a book or a game or a musical instrument. But it was some-
place that was all about you, in which you learned on your
own, grew on your own, without another's demands or expectations or influence directly affecting you.

Without such places, as children or as adults, we lose our
sense of self and of self-worth. I write this as a mix of introvert and extrovert. I believe even the most extroverted of us
have hidden-away places where others are not allowed to
come—in our mind, our heart, our body, perhaps in our
memories or our dreams. Maybe it's as simple an "alone
thing" as washing our hair or walking the dog.

Without spaces there can be no such places. We need
"wasted" space in our schedules and surroundings that offer
us sanctuary, us alone. I've known people who are afraid to
be alone, and there are times when I am afraid to be alone.
We would properly worry about someone who wanted to be

alone all the time. But to be "all-one," from which "alone" de-
rives, we sometimes need to be "set apart" from others, the
meaning of holy in Hebrew scripture, or "called out," the
meaning of the Christian scriptural word for church.

Throughout the years, I have had many "sanctuaries" to
which I retreated alone. At Yale, it was the tiny prayer chapel
underneath the main chapel of the Divinity School and my
"morning coffee with God" on the back porch of my student
housing. In Philadelphia I escaped to the horticultural garden on the University of Pennsylvania campus, or to the
banks of the Schulkyll River in Fairmount Park. Southern
California gave me a sanctuary as grand as the palisades
along the shoreline and as simple as a chair in my apartment,
set in front of a picture window that framed greenery. Atlanta
blessed me with a deck that looks out on a kudzu-covered
ravine filled with tall old trees that proliferate within the city.

More recently I have created a little meditation garden,
perhaps an unconscious response to recent terrorist attacks
on the United States. It is a tiny corner of my sloping back-
yard, terraced with stones, cloistered by a hedge, centered on
a young maple, appointed with star junipers and mondo grass
and flowers rising from a carpet of pine bark chips. While two
gargoyles keep guard at the entrances, a stone Celtic cross sits
on the ground in the center of my view, a wooden bench that
faces the upward slope. The dogs are learning I don't throw
balls for them from there. The bigger one, Calvin, has taken to
sitting like a gargoyle himself at one entrance; and Hobbes,
the smaller and codependent one, lies at my feet.

Spiritual necessity makes discovering or creating such
spaces easy and vital.

ᦕ HELP ME FIND MY PLACE FOR ESCAPE AND YET DEEPER INTIMACY
AND INVOLVEMENT.

The more deeply you live your spiritual
life, the easier it will be to discern the
difference between living with God and
living without God, and the easier it will
be to move away from the places where
God is no longer with you.

The Inner Voice of Love, 23

Though those closest to Henri have told me he continued to
have his ups and downs, it seemed to me that Henri's final
year was his happiest. In phone calls and faxes and one
overnight visit, Henri told me that he was better able to receive the love that friends offered him, friends with whom he
could be fully himself. He was blessed that his final year of
life was a sabbatical, and his posthumously published journal, *Sabbatical Journey,* is filled with time spent with friends
and family and spiritual communities, as well as books that
he described with enthusiasm that would never make the
Vatican reading list. He was finding those sanctuaries where
God loved, inspired, and revitalized him.

Our last visit was our most delightful. I had been encouraging him to come to Atlanta just for fun, and he made
plans to come in May of 1996. I asked if he minded dogs, and
he said, no, as long as our conversation was not just about
dogs: "I often find that people prefer to talk about their pets
rather than themselves!" His visit was delayed and shortened
by the death of a friend's father whose funeral he attended
in Chicago. I met him at the airport. That sunny spring af-
ternoon we visited on the deck. I prepared an elaborate plat-

ter of a variety of crackers, cheeses, and fruits and opened my finest bottle of wine (not nearly as fine as the occasional $200 bottles he was given by others!). I knew how much hospitality meant to him. He took us to dinner and regaled us with stories of his latest adventures, including one about a wealthy friend having him flown from Santa Fe to San Diego "for lunch" in her private jet! (This part of the story did not appear in his book, though the lunch did. Maybe it was cut because editors felt it made Henri appear too worldly, or, more likely, too childlike in his wonder and glee at such extravagance!)

The ease of our visit was quite a contrast to our earlier relationship! A few days ago I reread our correspondence. I found a particularly intimate exchange of letters between us in which I had felt him too emotionally demanding on a visit and he had felt I was too distant. Our friendship weathered that dissonance, thank God, and finally we could offer one another a sanctuary of mutual love and intimacy, where God was.

Sunday morning he led us in prayers on the deck. How much more meaningful this was for us than "going to church" together. One day in his home a local pastor called to ask him to be involved in something for the parish. Henri declined, explaining afterwards to me, to my surprise, that he was careful in his commitments to the church, lest he be caught up in a political and bureaucratic morass "where God is no longer with you," in the words of today's quote.

Maybe that's the realization of later life: the church becomes for us the network of friends who welcome you, pray with you, prompt you to think, challenge you, share charitable efforts, and work with you for justice.

ॐ **DEAR GOD, BLESS ME WITH DISCERNMENT TO FIND THE PLACES AND PEOPLE AND CIRCUMSTANCES WHERE I FIND YOU.**

In working for peace we may make a
certain division of the world between the forces
of light and the forces of darkness, and if that
happens I feel uneasy, mainly because I think that
each of us participates in both worlds. Then I ask
myself if such polarization prevents a creative
dialogue with the government, the army, and other
power groups, and if the "civil disobedience"
model is the most fruitful for our decade.

Sabbatical Journey, 153

Henri's reflections come in the midst of a visit with two friends who joined the Berrigan brothers in protests for which they were arrested and jailed. Henri is not ambivalent about his personal support of these friends, support he has given the Berrigans themselves, but is ambivalent about the nature of their witness.

Being part of a demonstration is a wonderful witness to what one believes. Going forward at an altar call to publicly witness one's belief in Jesus Christ was part of my upbringing. My political involvement also required public demonstrations: against the Vietnam war, racism, sexism, heterosexism, other forms of injustice, nuclear testing and proliferation, environmental harm, and, within the church, against the exclusion of lesbian, gay, bisexual, and transgender people.

But I am also aware of the self-righteousness and ego-satisfaction that comes with such public displays, and how easy it is for many to feel that they have actually "done" something, when demonstrations should only be the visible tip of the iceberg of reform for those truly committed to justice. And I am aware of the superiority over the opposition that many of us feel in the glory of a just cause, a moral superiority that makes dialogue as impossible as the opposition's moral superiority.

Reared in a fundamentalist home and church and school, I find myself resisting what I call a "liberal fundamentalism" that requires one to hold views deemed unquestionable by the justice movement. Having been an evangelical and then a social gospel proponent, a conservative Republican as a child and a liberal Democrat all my adult life, I see the values and liabilities of each camp. I remember Henri, addressing hundreds attending a Peace Fellowship breakfast at a national gathering of Presbyterians, courageously but gently including our need "to protect the rights of the unborn," a view too readily dismissed by liberals.

Maggie Kuhn, founder of the Grey Panthers, spoke years ago at a breakfast supporting gay rights. By the end of her rousing talk, she had our fists in the air, chanting, "No more nukes, no more nukes." Carried away with personal support for Maggie, my fist was raised, though my chant was not enthusiastic. I believe nuclear energy is more environmentally sound than petroleum and easier and cheaper than other forms of energy, especially in developing nations. But my pragmatism does not fit a certain ideological legalism.

The television program *West Wing* offers examples of thinking outside our respective ideological boxes. Discussing gun control, which I favor, one character stunned me by saying to her opponent, "It's not that you dislike guns—it's that you dislike the people who have them!" In other words, it's also a class issue. We don't like so-called "rednecks" who feel compelled to have guns. Though I still believe in gun control, I can't ride my high-horse quite as high as before.

Thus, when Henri implies his misgivings of our own "just war" in working for peace and justice, his words resonate with many of us in that struggle as we consciously check ourselves for hidden weapons.

༄ DISARM ME, GOD, OF AN UNQUESTIONED SELF.

You have never felt completely safe
in your body. But God wants to love you in all
that you are, spirit and body. . . . How then do
you bring your body home? By letting it participate in your deepest desire to receive and
offer love. Your body needs to be held and to
hold, to be touched and to touch.

The Inner Voice of Love, 19

An imagined dualism of spirit and body haunts Christianity. Because the spirit is obviously important in spirituality, the body is often held suspect, even in the most fashionably new expressions of spirituality. But if spirituality is ultimately about connection and relatedness, there is integrity of body and spirit. A true spiritual discipline should not be about disciplining the body, but about cultivating the integral relationship—the integrity—of spirit and body. That's more challenging than simply disciplining our bodies. It means understanding, as Henri wrote, "Not only do you *have* a body . . . but you *are* your body" (*Adam,* 49).

Many of us have not felt safe in our bodies. Our bodies have been judged by others. Our bodies have limitations and disabilities. Our bodies are the "wrong" color or gender. Our bodies have the "wrong" sexual orientation, or we do not fit our body gender. Our bodies have been abused or exploited. Our bodies have experienced violence or violation, illness or accident. Our bodies are truly vulnerable, and there's good reason not to feel completely safe in them.

But this is not the kind of insecurity Henri is speaking of. Henri is speaking as a celibate desperately hungry for physical intimacy, and here I don't use "physical intimacy" as a euphemism for sex, though I believe all physical proximity has erotic ramifications. I am using eros in its broadest application: that force that impels us toward union with another, whether with God or another human being.

And yet, as a celibate, Henri speaks for all of us who, at one time or another, have hungered for a physical relationship that was not possible. Perhaps we had or have difficulty making that kind of connection. Maybe professional boundaries restrained us, perhaps vocations or reputations held us in check. Death or divorce or departure of a significant other may have inhibited us. Fear of disease or desire or emotional intimacy comes into play. Age may be a factor, too young or too old. A sexual experience itself may leave us hungry to be held.

We have almost all been left alone on an evening preferring to be in the arms of someone who cared about us enough to caress us as they would a beloved pet! Passing of the peace in church doesn't quite cut it, nor does the hug therapist prescription of "twelve hugs a day" match a half-hour of holding.

That's what Henri wanted. To be held. To bring his body "home," of which he often writes, is to bring his body home to God. God is somehow incarnated in another's welcoming touch. No wonder that the embrace of the forgiving father in Rembrandt's painting of the prodigal served for Henri as an icon of God's touch, bringing him home to his body!

God touches us with tender loving care, making us feel safe, at home in our bodies, through a variety of icons and sacramentals. For some, it is another human being. For others, it is beloved pets or plants. It may be wrapping ourselves in a grandmother's quilt, sitting in a father's chair, keeping a daughter's doll on your desk, holding the family Bible. God may bring us home to our bodies through so many things for those with nerves to feel.

ᐦ **GIVE ME NERVE TO FEEL YOUR TOUCH IN EVERYTHING, O GOD.**

A new spirituality is being born in you.
Not body denying or body indulging but
truly incarnational.

The Inner Voice of Love, 32

Henri writes what could be our "mantra for the day" under the rubric, "Seek a New Spirituality," in his most angst-ridden journal. The entry represents a frustrating part of Henri. Despite his many personal revelations, sometimes, under the guise of intimacy, in this case verbal, Henri could actually impart very little information about himself while appearing to welcome you into his inner thoughts. What does he mean by "body denying" and "body indulging" in his personal life? The reader—or at least, this reader—can't tell whether he's embracing his celibate vocation or is questioning its restrictions. To write so enigmatically is either the work of a spiritual master or the necessity of a priest in a conservative church or the editorial efforts of a publisher concerned about Henri's marketability.

Nonetheless, today's quote is quotable and useful for readers' consideration. Whatever it meant to Henri at the time, what does it mean to you? What does it mean to be neither "body denying" nor "body indulging" in your own spirituality? What does it mean for you to be "truly incarnational"?

What is it like to be Christ in our relationships, to be God-like in how we treat others? The apostle Paul argued against sexual sin and spiritual sin on this basis. If we are the Body of Christ, he argued, how could we join Christ's body to a prostitute? In other words, how could we exploit another's body in that way? Or how could Christ's body behave unfaithfully? Or to take the analogy to one of the significant problems of today:

how could Christ's body abuse another body—verbally, emotionally, physically, sexually, spiritually? (The ordering here is by no means to suggest a hierarchy of abuse!)

Paul's rejection of "sins of the flesh" was not a rejection of sexual sin, but rather a rejection of *anything*—spiritual, sexual, whatever—that places ourselves over against God. And the concept of "antichrist" is useful in considering anything we do or do not do that opposes Christ.

Many of us have recited the prayer that confesses sins of commission or omission. But the truth is, when it comes to the body, Christians seem to focus on sins of commission rather than omission, though the latter is the way we most frequently act contrary to Christ.

I was preparing for a retreat when an apparently homeless man knocked on my front door asking for work. Most who read this will understand and even justify my sin of omission. I told him I wished him well, but explained I needed no work, sending him on his way.

Now, if I were truly incarnational, if I were truly of Christ, I would have invited him in, offered him a shower, given him some of my clothes, fed him, and welcomed him to stay in my guest room.

Churches often reach out to the homeless, a sign of a truly incarnational ministry. At the same time, most churches do what I did with this homeless man: they reject the spiritually homeless. And just as our secular economy systematically contributes to the problem of homelessness, our spiritual economy systematically contributes to the creation of a spiritually homeless class—those condemned by and excluded from the church.

Jesus gave his body to the spiritually homeless of his day. And the apostle Paul condemned as unworthy those who received Christ's flesh and blood while overlooking the Body excluded from the table (1 Corinthians 11:29).

∾ I WAS A STRANGER, AND YOU WELCOMED ME. (MATTHEW 25:35)

A seed only flourishes by staying in the
ground in which it is sown. When you keep
digging the seed up to check whether it is
growing, it will never bear fruit.

The Inner Voice of Love, 31

Ministry is like the seed that Henri describes in *The Inner Voice of Love.* We like to be in control, to see anticipated results from our actions. We keep checking for growth—or rather, what we deem growth.

But in *The Inner Voice,* Henri is speaking of himself. The minister—every Christian—is like a seed that is planted, trusting God's providence. "Unless a grain of wheat falls into the earth and dies, it remains just a single grain; but if it dies, it bears much fruit," Jesus said (John 12:24). As we lose our life to save it for the sake of the kingdom, we welcome God to work within us.

Ken Feit, a Jesuit-turned-clown who came to Yale at Henri's suggestion, traveled from place to place to perform his ministry. In my small discussion group for Henri's class, one of the students envied his freedom. Another remarked that Feit was not entirely free. Because of his travels, she explained, he was not free to enter long-term, day-to-day, intimate relationships.

When I was considering leaving a parish ministry after almost ten years, Henri advised me that ten years was long enough to stay in any one place. The longest he himself stayed anywhere professionally was ten years, and only twice: Yale and Toronto's Daybreak. Even in those places he traveled far and wide, for weeks at a time.

Henri's insight about finally being planted was hard won. Henri moved around so much that many people thought he was a member of an order rather than a diocesan priest, who is "incarnated" in his diocese of ordination and is less mobile. As much as Henri believed in an "incarnational" ministry, he didn't let it freeze him in one location. Being from the more laissez-faire Dutch church helped, as his bishop let him take assignments all over North and South America, with the permission and under the auspices of local bishops.

The Spirit blows where it will, and undoubtedly it was sometimes the Spirit leading Henri to new growth, but equally undoubtedly, it was sometimes just plain ol' Henri reaching out to new interests and fresh communities. When I first knew him, he seemed firmly rooted at Yale. On a visit there after his death, it was hard to believe that Henri was not still there on the hill in his apartment on campus.

Henri did not firmly root himself again until Daybreak, the L'Arche community of Toronto, where he "experienced a sense of at-homeness [he] had not experienced at Yale, in Latin America, or at Harvard" (*Road to Daybreak*, 4). The community invited him to make his home with them, a far cry from all previous invitations simply to work. That's why, though Henri died in his homeland of Holland, his family brought his body home to Daybreak. Instead of being buried next to his beloved mother, he would be buried surrounded by members of the family that adopted him. Who knows what fruit he might have borne had he had more time to blossom there! But his legacy is firmly planted there, and the Henri Nouwen Literary Centre as well as the community's chapel Dayspring have both sprung from his willingness as a seed to be planted, and thus flourish.

༄ THINK ABOUT YOURSELF AS A LITTLE SEED PLANTED IN RICH SOIL. ALL YOU HAVE TO DO IS STAY THERE AND TRUST THAT THE SOIL CONTAINS EVERYTHING YOU NEED TO GROW. (*INNER VOICE*, 31)

When [Theodore] Roszak describes the
shaman, he describes at the same time the service
every minister and priest should offer: to be like an
"artist, who lays his work before the community in
the hope that through it, as through a window,
the reality he has fathomed can be witnessed by
all who give attention" (Theodore Roszak,
The Making of a Counter-Culture
[New York: Doubleday, 1969]).

Creative Ministry, 104

In his biography on Henri entitled *Wounded Prophet,* British journalist Michael Ford makes the point that Henri was a popularizer, a writer who interpreted for the general public difficult concepts of the scholars whose books lined his shelves. Henri's writings are sprinkled with insightful quotes from others such as the one above that easily validate Ford's observation. Yet what is also true but less apparent is that Henri's deceptively simple ways of putting things belie his erudition. His words emerge not only from his heart and personal experience, but from a mind like Coleridge's that deftly grasped and blended his biblical, philosophical, theological, psychological, historical, cultural, and spiritual studies. He was as passionate a student as he was a teacher, exemplified by being the only Yale professor I ever witnessed auditing a divinity course in which I was enrolled myself.

Henri's "art" as a shaman has been carefully crafted. When the great cathedrals of Europe were built, the vast majority of the people were illiterate. But they learned the stories of faith through the work of artisans who created sculptures, bas reliefs, paintings, and stained glass windows. I think of Henri as a contemporary maker of stained glass windows that proclaim the gospel "reality he has fathomed" through research and prayer to those of us who haven't the time, inclination, or education to research ourselves. A Baptist minister put it this way: he viewed himself as paid by his congregation to take the time to read a little more and listen a little more, reflecting back in sermons the spiritual growth and insights of the church at large and his congregation in particular.

On the worship committee at Yale Divinity School, I became very passionate in a debate as to whether the worship leader should be a transparent window to God (*a la* Tillich) or, as I argued, one whose personality was apparent, who was "there." After all, God was the God of Abraham and Sarah, of Moses, and of Miriam, and so on. I had grown up in a "low" church setting in which charismatic and "personal" leadership was expected. I was arguing with those from "high" church settings in which it was anticipated the priest would seem to disappear. These days I would argue that spiritual leadership needs to be both, a clear window to God as well as a stained glass window that tells a personal story.

My last name indicates an ancestor of mine was a glassmaker. Maybe it's in my genes, but the most interesting clear glass to me is that in which you can see imperfections that reveal the glassmaker's human hand. The most moving stained glass windows are those in which the colors are diverse and intense. As a shaman, Henri was both kinds of glass: stained and beautiful, clear and flawed. In my view, churches need both kinds of glass.

ᔕ **Stained and beautiful, clear and flawed, may others see in my window your light, O God!**

There was a time when silence
was normal and a lot of racket disturbed us.
But today, noise is the normal fare,
and silence, strange as it may seem,
has become the real disturbance.

With Open Hands, 36

Unprovidentially today, when there is silence in worship it most often means that someone has missed his cue in the liturgy or lost her place in the sermon. If time is set aside for silence, such as to pray individual confessions of sin, it must not be so long as to lose the "pace" of worship.

"Successful" churches thrive on filling up their worshipers with inspirational music and uplifting words. Praise choruses are popular, the bigger the choir the better, the more dramatic the soloist the grander. Scriptures should be short and few, the preacher should shout the message from the rooftops, as it were. And it should all be very affirming— for the chosen, that is. Sometimes megachurches are to spirituality what "big food" is to cuisine.

Churches are competing for our attention with the media's unrelenting bombardment of action, soundtracks, laugh tracks, sound bites, instant analysis, personalities, and hype. Silence in movie theaters, on television, and on the radio is the occasion of an apology for "technical difficulties."

Thus in personal devotions we need silence all the more. The most vital portion of my own morning prayer is the silence, quieting both chatter of the mind and passions of the heart to listen to absolutely nothing. Sometimes the silence seems so thick I am rendered immobile. Sometimes the silence is so light I feel like I might float out of the chair. Strangely, mysteriously, there is a comforting Presence in that silence, which I believe is God. I don't believe God comes to me because of my silence. I believe God is always there, and my silence allows me awareness of that presence.

Elijah heard God's voice not in a wind, fire, or earthquake, but in the "sound of sheer silence" (1 Kings 19:12). After the storms, fires, and earthquakes of our lives, we, too, may be attentive to God in silence. If I let even my prayers or the scriptures interfere with this silence with God, I miss the whole point of the exercise. Think of the comfortable silences into which a child may fall with a parent, or a friend with a friend, or a lover with the beloved. These are among the finest moments of life.

At a retreat I heard its leader speak of how we "get hooked into other peoples' stories" through the media instead of attending to our own stories. My first reaction to the speaker's words was that I don't want to be selfish or lack compassion. And yet I realize how the media exercise my emotions, pulling me to and fro, throwing me off center, even as I begin my day. My morning prayer that follows brings me back to what's vital.

❧ I HOLD MYSELF IN QUIET AND SILENCE, LIKE A LITTLE CHILD IN ITS MOTHER'S ARMS. (PSALM 131:2, NJB)

Jesus' appearance in our midst
has made it undeniably clear that
changing the human heart and changing
human society are not separate tasks,
but are as interconnected as the two
beams of the cross.

The Wounded Healer, 20

Every time we walk into a church, we should be reminded of the need for the Body of Christ to be involved in the body politic. We are faced with the cross, the means of political execution for those who challenged Rome. If Jesus had been killed for religious reasons, he would have been stoned to death. For those who face a crucifix, the body of Jesus still hangs on that cross, a reminder of the suffering not only of Christ but of the whole world even today. For those who face an empty cross, it may serve as a reminder that God's desire is for resurrection and abundant living for us all.

Opponents to the civil rights movement in the United States of the last century claimed "you can't legislate love." Of course they missed the point. Civil rights isn't about changing hearts, it's about changing laws and patterns of law enforcement so people are treated equitably—equal rights, not "special" rights. It's about form rather than content. Form can influence content, of course. As more black Americans were able to vote, to sit with white Americans at lunch counters and on buses, to be educated and work and live and play alongside the majority, hearts were inevitably changed. But the lingering racism in most cultures that now ensure civil rights proves that changing society neither automatically nor entirely changes the human heart.

Jesus' crucifixion by Rome radically changed the movement that would bear his name. The "ultimate solution" failed, and resulted in changing the Roman Empire rather than the other way around, as that empire was gradually Christianized. The crucifixion still changes people's hearts, as they recognize within Christ's suffering God's compassion for the whole of humanity.

A visit with victims of the United States' Central American policies in Nicaragua changed Henri's heart. Hearing the pain and suffering inflicted by the U.S.-funded and equipped contras on the loved ones of the women of Jalapa, one of the Americans in Henri's group asked the women, "Can you forgive us?" A woman replied, "Yes, we forgive you." The question was put and answered in several different ways, and soon Henri was "lifted up in this litany of forgiveness." Henri saw "the broken heart of the dying Christ" stretched out on the crossbeam of Central America. (Based on *Christ of the Americas: Dying and Rising and Coming Again* [pamphlet], 11–14, and on a 1982 presentation in Pasadena, California.)

✎ THANK YOU FOR ENTERING HUMAN SUFFERING WITH SACRED PURPOSE: FORGIVENESS AND REDEMPTION.

When you discover in yourself
something that is a gift from God,
you have to claim it and not let it be
taken away from you.

The Inner Voice of Love, 44

Through the ages, saints and martyrs have borne witness to gifts derided or decried by others, including the church: Joan of Arc's voices, John of the Cross's visions, Francis of Assisi's poverty and stigmata, Sir Thomas More's unyielding justice, Teresa of Avila's voices and visions, Martin Luther's tower experiences and Reformation. Contemporary Christian saints have similarly claimed their gifts, challenging society: Dorothy Day, Martin Luther King Jr., Cesar Chavez, Oscar Romero, Mother Teresa, Rosemary Radford Ruether, and Troy Perry, to name a few who welcomed their gifts from God and claimed them, resisting those who would deny God's gracious acts in their lives.

Probably all of us have gifts from God that others doubt or question. In college, one of my favorite professors, a Lutheran pastor, told students that his father still asked when he was going to get "a real job." A friend in Philadelphia who was both gay and an artist told me it was more difficult to "come out" to his family as an artist than as a gay man! When I am asked what I do and explain that I am a writer, I often see eyes glaze over even before I tell them the content of my writings. A friend who is a full-time mother gets the same treatment.

In every way like us, Henri was buffeted by people who challenged him on many fronts. Should he deny his sexuality and his need for an intimate companion? Should he deny his vocation as a priest and his call to celibacy? Should he deny his spirituality to teach "academic" courses that objectify faith? Should he deny his love of van Gogh or Rembrandt to teach more recognizable spiritual guides? Should he deny the joy and fulfillment he experienced working with mentally disabled people and their assistants? Should he deny his gift to simplify complex spiritual issues in his writings to pursue a more scholarly approach?

Meditating on *The Inner Voice of Love,* the reader might forget that the spiritual imperatives that title each meditation and the meditations themselves were not devised for readers. Henri was addressing himself in a journal that he never intended to publish. So, in this entry, he is admonishing himself to claim God's gifts in him.

Often, if not usually, we admonish others for things we are struggling with in ourselves. For example, I can see perfectionist tendencies or control issues in others because I see them in myself. Sometimes we do this unawares. Henri models for us in this journal a way of approaching our own "reformation," our own "conversion." After all, prayer is the place of conversion, as the Desert Fathers and Mothers believed. In our own prayer time and spiritual journaling, we may say or write to ourselves what spiritual concerns we are addressing.

For many people, spirituality or religion is about correction. But equally the case, spirituality and religion is about affirmation. In our spiritual disciplines, we need to claim our gifts, even those others may not recognize or value.

ᑄ THANK YOU FOR ALL YOUR GIFTS TO ME, ESPECIALLY THOSE THAT MAKE ME UNIQUELY ME AND OFFER ME DISTINCTIVE PERSPECTIVES AND OPPORTUNITIES. MAY I USE THEM IN YOUR SERVICE AND THE SERVICE OF OTHERS.

"STANDING UNDER" RATHER THAN UNDERSTANDING GRIEF

The endless dialogue,
"I am sorry" . . . "Yes, I am sad,"
often touches off a strange weariness
instead of bringing comfort.

In Memoriam, 9

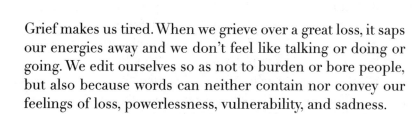

Grief makes us tired. When we grieve over a great loss, it saps our energies away and we don't feel like talking or doing or going. We edit ourselves so as not to burden or bore people, but also because words can neither contain nor convey our feelings of loss, powerlessness, vulnerability, and sadness.

Henri writes about his mother's death, the pain of which I could only imagine when I first read *In Memoriam.* But the book was a very great comfort after my own mother's death two decades later. I sent copies to my brother and sister because I hoped it would comfort them as it did me when I reread it.

Henri writes of the experience as not being unique, but again expresses the refrain "what is most universal is also most personal" (*In Memoriam,* 10). He knows it will touch the pang of loss in others' hearts whose mothers have died.

Yet in examining this particular grief, the loss of a mother, Henri's experience and our own become even more universally applicable to all of our losses. Like the Eastern practice of spiritual novitiates watching a corpse decompose to take in (rather than understand or even comprehend) all mutability, so being attentive to a particular grief makes us attentive to the nature of grief. And a part of each "little" grief is its reminder of the cumulative grief every person carries over a lifetime.

The loss of a friend, a vocation, a home, a pet, a marriage, a job, retirement funds—the list could go on and on (you may wish to add your own losses here)—all are occasions for grief, all make us weary, all make us wary of our "investments." Beyond our individual losses, we endure collective losses if we are members of a marginalized group, an economically deprived community, a neighborhood destroyed by a disaster, a group struggling with a disease, or a nation suffering terrorism or war or poverty or hunger.

What I've experienced in times of great loss is that rarely could I find someone who could hold my feelings, simply hold my feelings. Because of my leadership roles in the church, it was difficult for many to see me at a loss. They needed to put me back together again, in a hurry.

All of us have heard facile advice, like "it won't seem so bad later" or "look at the silver lining" or "it could be worse" or "other people suffer more." Henri said in presentations that comparing your suffering to that of others doesn't help, because your suffering is your own. I think it is better for us to *guard* one another's feelings in the midst of grief rather than *guide* one another's feelings. Talking about it, praying about it, and writing about it somehow relieves the welling grief that each of us holds. And then, silence needs to follow. A welcoming silence. A silence that understands. In Camus' conceptualization, true understanding is "standing under," receiving without being in control (as understanding or "superior" knowledge often implies). Just as standing under rain or sunshine, so we need to "stand under" our own or another's feelings.

掘 KEEP ME FROM TRYING TO CATCH MY FEELINGS OF GRIEF, OR ANOTHER'S FEELINGS OF GRIEF. LET THE FEELINGS FLOW THROUGH MY HEART AND HANDS, AND THEN INTO YOUR HEART AND HANDS.

I have a deep sense,
hard to articulate, that if we could
really befriend death we would be free
people. So many of our doubts and
hesitations, ambivalences and
insecurities are bound up with our
deep-seated fear of death.

A Letter of Consolation, 30–31

"To befriend" is a phrase Henri attributes to Jungian analyst and teacher James Hillman, who used it in the sense of embracing the shadows of our experience as well as the light. Befriending death is like befriending grief, giving it a hospitable place simply to be held. Just as we "stand under" grief, we must "stand under" death, receiving without being in control. Henry writes in this letter to his father on the occasion of his mother's death that "Befriending death seems to be the basis of all other forms of befriending. . . . Fear of death often drives us into death, but by befriending death, we can face our mortality and choose life freely" (*A Letter of Consolation,* 29, 30–31).

Henri wonders in the letter if, despite the many deaths his father had endured, the death of his love of forty-seven years took him by surprise "because love — deep, human love — does not know death." He may as well have quoted the Song of Solomon: "For love is as strong as death, passion fierce as the grave" (Song of Solomon 8:6).

As mentioned earlier, when asked about the afterlife on a Dutch radio program, Henri's father (who outlived his son) basically responded, "We'll see." I confess to the same limited faith (or unlimited faith, depending on your point of view), a trust that God knows what's best regarding our individual existence. But I do know that my mother and father and my spiritual "father" Henri live. After each died, I felt them in my chest, strengthening and cheering me on. My experience with Henri came as my plane ascended from a rainswept Toronto after his funeral mass. Somehow I felt resolve and certainty of my belovedness and calling. What could anyone do to me now? And once my mother died, the last of my three spiritual guides to do so, I believed I had experienced the worst that death could do (after all, no one has or will love me as long and as well as she did)—and yet my soul was not vanquished. All three of them are still with me and within me.

James B. Nelson has written that writers write about that with which they struggle. Interestingly, Henri's letter of consolation to his father is as much a letter to himself. And it's not just consolation in the loss of his mother, but consolation in the earlier absence of his father. It's another reaching out from Henri, this time to a parent who had formerly let the mother take care of the personal "stuff" of their relationship. Now his father had stepped forward and a new relationship was being born for them both. Henri acknowledges this as a blessing in the midst of the curse, not only in relation to his father, but to his siblings as well. In my own life, my mother's death brought my brother and sister and me together in a new way, no longer able to use Mom as a relay station for our personal messages to one another.

ℭ **EVEN THOUGH I WALK THROUGH THE VALLEY OF THE SHADOW OF DEATH, I FEAR NO EVIL; FOR THOU ART WITH ME. (PSALM 23:4, RSV).**

Physical and spiritual closeness
are two quite different things, and they
can—although they do not always—
inhibit each other.

A Letter of Consolation, 21

Most of us have friends with whom, after lengthy periods apart, we can resume the relationship just where we left off. Others of us have met people who became friends almost immediately, as if we've known them our whole lives. And family members who enjoyed close relationships growing up together know each other well enough to sense in one another's voices over the phone nuances of changes that may go unobserved by those nearer at hand. Classmates, army buddies, coworkers, family (biological and nonbiological), former girlfriends or boyfriends or spouses, and still others may all play the role of friends of our soul, our timeless identity. They can see (and we let them see) something in us others cannot, something beloved, an inner self.

Sometimes these "soul friends" can know something's up without apparent communication, like a friend from another state who called a year since we had last spoken, concerned because she had dreamed I committed suicide. It was uncanny, because I was, in fact, going through a very rough time, and her expression of care really buoyed me up when I felt myself sinking.

One of my most remarkable experiences of intimacy with old friends came when a former classmate organized the first reunion for our ninth grade, class of 1965, some twenty-seven years after our graduation. We got together for a weekend at a hotel along the beach in Santa Barbara, interestingly, without spouses so we didn't have to explain anything to those who didn't share our experience of attending a strict fundamentalist Christian school. Most of us had not seen each other since we departed for various public high schools.

Given our original context, I wondered if they would accept who I am today. They did. We accepted each other because we had been through something together, both wonderful and awful. The teacher most laughed at when we were kids was the one we remembered most fondly as adults. We learned we all had the same discomfort with another teacher, who touched students inappropriately. We discovered that we were grateful for the educational discipline we had received which had led each of us into interesting lives. We also realized how bonded we were by the trauma and trivia of the narrow view of the world afforded those who are religiously rigid. When I left the gathering, I cried. I felt as if I were leaving home. Typical of me, I wanted to write a book about my classmates, but that hasn't happened yet. What's strange is that we haven't repeated the experience. Maybe it's just enough to know we still belong to one another, that none of us were "crazy" in our personal interpretation of that childhood experience. Maybe it's just enough to know we loved each other. Remembering them, I can be reassured that the inner voice that tells me I am loveable and loving is not misguided.

Henri told the story of a student moving a great distance who wanted to say goodbye. After sitting together for a long time in silence, the student offered him this valediction: "From now on, all ground between us is holy ground." Spiritual intimacy transmutes even distance into sacred space.

ᐤ **THANKS BE TO GOD FOR FAMILY AND FRIENDS WHO REINFORCE MY SENSE OF BELONGING, WORTHY OF LOVE AND ABLE TO LOVE, EVEN AT A DISTANCE.**

I can say that [my mother] gave me
that basic sense of the goodness of life
that allowed me to move freely and
fearlessly to many places, to live with
many different people and in many
different circumstances, and to
feel free far from home.

In Memoriam, 34–35.

Previously I quoted the New Jerusalem Bible's translation of Psalm 131:2, but the New Revised Standard Version renders it this way: "But I have calmed and quieted my soul, like a weaned child with its mother; my soul within me is like a weaned child." (The very last phrase is a footnote alternative.)

A child that is weaned no longer needs the mother's milk, but is able to eat other foods. This means the child is no longer absolutely dependent on its mother. The mother is relieved of a sometimes uncomfortable and even painful method of feeding, and the child is freer to roam farther from Mother. This is an extraordinary spiritual metaphor for our relationship with God and our experience of the spiritual life. As we develop our spiritual life, we too can move out from God's lap, from safety and security, to others and to adventures yet to be revealed.

Henri writes about his own mother's love, whose unconditional nature made it possible for him to leave her without accusations of abandonment, inattention, or disloyalty. Many mothers are not "ideal" in this way, but become possessive and demanding of their children. I experienced my own mother's love as Henri did his, giving me a strong sense of independent identity that enabled me to go far from the nest in my travels and in establishing a home. Yet I knew my mother was conflicted. Like Jesus, a mother hen who wanted to gather her brood to herself, she also wanted to be close to her children. The night before she unexpectedly died, I phoned her from my home in Atlanta to tell her I was going to see Hal Holbrook's one-man show, performing as Mark Twain. When I returned home to California for her funeral, I found on her reading table a book of quotes from Mark Twain, with a bookmark in the middle. Apparently she had decided to join me vicariously in the performance, and I was touched. Her love had made me less dependent on her, but at the same time my late father's love, my love, and that of her ever-increasing family made her less dependent on us.

Perfect love frees us for life and for love. That's the love of God, knitting us together in our mother's womb (Psalm 139:13), comforting us "as a mother comforts her child . . . dandled on her knees" (Isaiah 66:13, 12), welcoming her brood home to the protection of her wings (Luke 13:34), and yet sending us off into the world with the reminder that "I am with you always, to the end of the age" (Matthew 28:20).

ↄ **May I enter that perfect love that makes fears dissipate in its wake.**

If I were to let my life be taken over
by what is urgent, I might very well never get
around to what is essential.

Letters to Marc, 3

Having just spent an hour on line dealing with e-mails whose very nature scream urgency, I heartily concur with Henri's sentiment. Most of these internet communications are junk mail or spam ("group mailings"), often from people whose names I barely recognize, forwarding jokes or sentimental stories or calls to action. They're neither personal nor essential. Paul McComas, a writer friend in Chicago, has purposely stayed off the internet so as not to be distracted from his writing. I've told him that this is clearly part of his monastic discipline! I too would adopt a noninternet lifestyle if I didn't need it for so much of my work.

Thus, timing of its use is important. I usually read e-mails later in the day, saving most of my creative energies for writing in the morning. But today I had to print out an e-mail giving me directions I need for someone else *now*. While on line, I couldn't resist knocking off some of my e-mails, deleting many without even opening them. But several seemed to require immediate action, and attending to them has made me feel hassled and harried. The glimpse of the internet has almost eclipsed the wonder of the "outer net" of the universe I felt privileged to glimpse as the sun rose during this morning's prayers.

Of course I write all of this to illustrate Henri's point. Discerning the spirits today requires delineating between what is essential and what is urgent. Admittedly, sometimes what is essential is urgent, like the Notre Dame professor Henri describes in *Out of Solitude* who always complained about all the interruptions to his work until he realized that his interruptions *were* his work! What I, too, discovered in parish ministry was that frequently I was reacting to things that came up, rather than being the now clichèd "proactive" person I wanted to be.

Henri contrasted reacting to responding, suggesting that a reaction comes from the mind and hands, while a response comes from the heart. To avoid becoming reactionaries, we have to let the events of our day descend from our minds to our hearts, just like the prayers of the Desert Fathers and Mothers. It is within the heart, close to God, that we may gain perspective on what's vital and what's not. (Of course, not everything is even worth the trouble of that descent!)

A friend in Hawaii has vowed never to eat fast food, to maintain the value of the dining experience—preparing the food (or waiting for it to be prepared), sitting at table, perhaps with a friend, savoring a meal, and giving thanks. This is applicable to every realm of life. It is what having sex is to making love, having a job is to having a vocation, channel surfing is to being involved in a story. Unprovidentially, too often we can make the comparison that it is also what religion is to spirituality.

When our religion is preoccupied with orthodoxy, morality, or politics, we may fail to "taste and see that the Lord is good" (Psalm 34:8).

ᐩ **HELP ME TO LIVE, TO REALLY LIVE THE LIFE OF BLESSINGS YOU HAVE PROMISED!**

When we are able to cast off
our fears and come close to the many who
have grown old, we see old men and
women telling stories to children with eyes
full of wonder and amazement.

Aging: The Fulfillment of Life, 59

Thus old people revitalize the world even as they may be losing their personal vitality, offering stories of humor, history, faith, endurance, experience, and love. Think how engrossed the world was when the film *Titanic* was released. The key to the fictional story lay in an old woman's memory. No cast of celebrities, no Hollywood extravagance, no special effects nor high-tech sound could have told the story without her.

As a young adult, I boldly "theorized" that the reason we require fewer experiences as we get older is because each occasion brings a flood of memories and associations that makes the simplest event rich with meaning. Today I realize that older people often enjoy a greater level of activity than do the young. Yet it is true that their past experience provides resonance, perspective, context, and content.

We are the children "with eyes full of wonder and amazement" even as adults as we welcome the stories of people whose senior ranks we ourselves are rapidly joining. It's true that some older people, like some younger people, are more interesting than others, depending on their attitudes toward life as much as how much life they have lived, whether within their minds through reading, within their families through rearing children, or within the world of adventure, wartime, calamity, or social unrest. And it's true that there is a shadow side of growing old, as Henri points out, that may allow us to stereotype and dismiss older people for their frailty, rigidity, complaints, pains, and fears. As the adage goes, "Getting old ain't for sissies!" The very fact that they have survived thus far indicates a strength about them that commands admiration.

Henri points out that a likely reason the old are ignored is our personal fear of the aging process. And today's marketplace, entertainment, and much religion is geared for the young. Even our prime model for living a Christian life died at the age of thirty-three. Once I confided to a minister nearing retirement that I found it difficult to completely identify with Jesus because so little is known of his sexuality. He responded that he found it difficult to relate to Jesus because he never had to endure old age.

How would Jesus have coped with the challenges of aging? Dying by littles is not as grand as martyrdom. How would he have handled challenges to his health, or worse, being forgotten by his followers? Henri used to speak of the necessity for Christ to be the way without getting in the way. His early departure allowed for the coming of the Spirit and the birth of the church. But what if he had been forced to retire?

There are different kinds of crosses, and Jesus had his own to bear. We who will age have a unique opportunity to witness our faith in old age. Until then, we can follow Jesus' lead of attending to the woman stooped with age in the synagogue, or the woman who suffered a hemorrhage for twelve years, or his own mother losing a son in a public execution. And we can learn from older followers of Jesus how to cope with aging.

ᐁ **BLESS ME WITH RESPECT FOR MY ELDERS, AND BLESS ME WITH RESPECT AS AN ELDER.**

When our unhealed wounds
determine the atmosphere around us,
we become anxious.

Turn My Mourning into Dancing, 14

Not only do we become anxious — those around us do, too.

We have all been around people whose wounds make us handle them with kid gloves. They may be volatile or easily hurt. They may have been treated unfairly or unjustly, been hurt by others or by circumstances. They may be part of groups that have been treated this way. We surely want to avoid "blaming the victim," but there are people who never become survivors, who never move beyond the pain, violence, abuse, abandonment, indignities, prejudice, and discrimination they have endured.

One step removed are those of us who identify with them or the persecuted groups to which they belong. Justice-seeking people may also be difficult to be around, sensitive to nuances of evil and injustice, sometimes to the point of imagining harm when none is intended. As George Eliot (née Mary Anne Evans) observed, "Notions and scruples were like spilt needles, making one afraid of treading, or sitting down, or even eating" (George Eliot, *Middlemarch*, Modern Library paperback ed., [New York: Random House, 2000], 17).

Do we want to emanate a merciless atmosphere around us that makes people afraid to say what they really think, express what they really feel, or be who they really are? Do we want honesty or duplicity? I know I have been silenced by those whose unforgiving air brooks no disagreement nor challenge. Undoubtedly I have silenced others in the same way.

As wounded healers, we must attend to our own wounds. We have "a wound with a view"—that is, we have the ability to see things in a different way, to learn from what has hurt us, to move beyond our woundedness to healing. If our wounds still smart, if we are too sensitive, we are less likely to bring healing, but instead will inflict wound for wound, an eye for an eye. If we are truly to love those who persecute us, to do good to them, then we are going to want to heal them too. To me this does not necessarily mean that we stay in abusive situations, either domestically, politically, or ecclesiastically. In fact, we need distance to heal and to be healing. Sometimes the distance needed is a lifetime.

But once out of an abusive or oppressive situation, we need to find healing that allows us to be in new relationships without prejudice. Few situations have been as unjust and brutal as apartheid, yet the new South Africa instituted a Commission on Truth and Reconciliation, which facilitated an airing of grievances and brutalities without retribution. For those of us who come from litigious cultures, this process seems incomprehensible. But for a nation that wants to get on with its life, it seems vital.

For people who want to get on with their lives, we too must move beyond our wounds. As Henri writes, "Facing our losses also means avoiding a temptation to see life as an exercise in having needs met" (*Turn My Mourning into Dancing*, 9). It is not that our wounds and our losses are not important, it's just that life is always an opportunity for learning, healing, and living.

ॐ TURN MY MOURNING INTO DANCING; TAKE OFF MY SACKCLOTH AND CLOTHE ME WITH JOY, SO THAT MY SOUL MAY PRAISE YOU AND NOT BE SILENT! (ADAPTED FROM PSALM 30:11–12)

When we mourn, we die to
something that gives us a sense of who
we are. In this sense suffering always has
much to do with the spiritual life.

Turn My Mourning into Dancing, 29

In this book that was published posthumously, Henri illustrates the concept of letting go by the flyers and catchers of the trapeze artists described in *Our Greatest Gift:* "Before they can be caught they must let go. They must brave the emptiness of space" (*Turn My Mourning,* 25). He speaks of "the call to hold our lives lightly," realizing that we are not totally in control. Novelist Milan Kundera called it "the unbearable lightness of being," his philosophical counterpoint to Nietzsche's myth of eternal return wherein repetition created life's heaviness, or substance. Both Nouwen and Kundera point to the fragility of life.

To most people, mourning and suffering are "heavy" emotions, burdening us, holding us down. But they are also a means by which we learn to let go. It's like falling into water encumbered with weighty clothing, baggage, possessions. To rise to the surface, to survive, we must let go of all that holds us down, who or what we mourn, why we suffer, even the mourning and suffering itself.

In the metaphor of trapeze flying, we must not cling to what we've known or where we've been or with whom. We must even let go of who we've been. We must "brave the emptiness of space," trusting someone will be there to catch us, that a new home awaits, that purpose will unveil itself. We travel the birth canal out of the womb more than once in life.

I have experienced hundreds of deaths of friends and acquaintances to AIDS, cancer, heart disease, other illnesses, accidents, and violence. What it has taught me is that life is precious, and yet ephemeral. The body is strong, but vulnerable. Death is fearful, yet not as frightening as it once was. Friends in the AIDS community especially speak of "visits" from those who have passed on, and a friend who studied and wrote on the paranormal told me that when human beings are confronted with the deaths of so many in a short span of time, the boundary between death and life seems quite permeable.

Of course we not only mourn the loss of people. We mourn the loss of vocations, callings, jobs, opportunities, pets, material possessions, security, and so forth. We suffer losses of health and well-being and safety and independence and a sense of belonging. What the experience may tell us is that we are more than all of those things: losing everything, we do not lose ourselves, whom God holds and loves eternally.

Writing of Søren Kirkegaard, Peter Drucker wrote, "Faith is not what today is so often called a 'mystical experience,' something that can apparently be induced by the proper breathing exercises or by prolonged exposure to Bach (not to mention drugs). It can be attained only through despair, through suffering, through painful and ceaseless struggle."

Those who think of spirituality as an easy way out or a form of denial do not understand its nature. As the adage goes, "Religion is for people afraid of going to hell. Spirituality is for people who have already been there."

෨ I LET GO OF ALL I THINK I CAN HOLD ONTO, AND I AM LIGHT AS A BUTTERFLY FLOATING IN AIR.

As long as we keep running around,
anxiously trying to affirm ourselves or be
affirmed by others, we remain blind to
One who has loved us first, dwells in our
heart, and has formed our truest self.

Turn My Mourning into Dancing, 32

Affirmations are big these days. Self-help gurus encourage us to make self-affirmations, success-oriented guides advise us to affirm others as well as ourselves. Positive reinforcement exercises help everyone from politicians to athletes. We are told to be good to ourselves when something bad happens: eat chocolate, go shopping, dine well, drink exquisite brandy. Meditation is viewed as simply one more channel for feeling good about ourselves.

But the spiritual path takes us deeper. Even without believing in God, the very fact that you are you is the refining result of the evolution of matter to life, and life to you. You are an accomplishment long before you accomplish anything. You're body is a grand result of an æons-long experiment. Your mind can do things no computer can do (at least yet!). Your feelings can fuel bonding and challenge injustice and inspire creations of your own.

For Christians, it is God's inspiration that has loved you into being. God's inspiration within your feelings, mind, and body. God's inspiration in the evolution to you from life, and to life from matter. That inspiration is the "first love" the author of 1 John writes about and Henri alludes to: "Not that we loved God but that [God] loved us" (1 John 4:10). The epistle writer further attests that the only reason we are able to love is because God loved us first.

Returning to that first love is spiritually essential. Jesus used the metaphor of himself as the vine and we as the branches. We must remain rooted in that first love or we cannot bear fruit. As necessary as it is to receive love from many sources—our parents, our children, our friends, our lovers— no love is so essential to remember, to bask in, to pleasure in, as that first love, the love of God.

Being the Beloved makes us more loving and more loveable.

The reason, Henri would say, that we are disappointed in love is because no other love can be as perfect and unconditional as the love that created us, compassionately embraces us, and empowers us to love. Creation, atonement, and inspiration are three different ways we can know God's love.

Even in the case of God's love we tend to search outside ourselves for its signs and manifestations. We see God in nature, in our relationships, in our work, in our play, in church or spiritual community, in justice, at home, in the many things with which we've been blessed. God is surely in all these things, but the greatest gift God has given you is you. Without those other blessings, God is still within you.

"But God, being rich in faithful love, through the great love with which [God] loved us, even when we were dead in our sins, brought us to life with Christ . . . We are God's work of art, created in Christ Jesus for the good works which God has already designated to make up our way of life." (Ephesians 2:4, 10, NJB)

So our creation and re-creation is love enough. Whatever other love comes our way is a bonus!

ᦡ I GIVE THANKS TO YOU, O GOD, FOR ME.

He is mother as well as father.
He touches the son with a masculine hand
and a feminine hand. He holds, and she
caresses. He confirms and she consoles.
He is, indeed, God, in whom both manhood
and womanhood, fatherhood and mother-
hood, are fully present.

The Return of the Prodigal Son, 94

Henri is describing the welcoming father in Rembrandt's painting, *The Return of the Prodigal Son.* He is not alone in noticing that one hand is masculine and the other is feminine; art scholars earlier confirmed his observation.

Early in my prayer life, during my morning prayer, which concludes with the prayer Jesus taught, I replaced "Our Father" with, "God, Mother and Father of us all." I did it not to correct a largely patriarchal religion, but because it felt right spiritually. That is, "Father" was an inadequate metaphor for me to use for God. I experienced God as Father and Mother. My change was one of spiritual necessity, though many Christians would be offended by my interpolation, especially in a prayer believed given us by Jesus himself!

Succeeding generations of the faithful have often made such necessary adjustments. The Bible itself records a shifting understanding of the nature of God. Early Christians did not hesitate to adapt and sometimes manipulate their own scriptures to proclaim their fresh experience of God in Jesus. In my book *Coming Out As Sacrament,* dedicated to Henri, I concluded that God comes out to us ultimately on the pages of scripture not as a violently coercive deity, but as a vulnerably persuasive God. Readers may discover this in Jewish scriptures ("For I desire steadfast love, not sacrifice" [Hosea 6:6]) even before it is presented in Christian scriptures.

Jack Miles, author of the Pulitzer-prize winning book *God: A Biography*, has continued his scholarly work in *Christ: A Crisis in the Life of God*. Though I think it problematic that he discusses the Bible as if it were a single literary narrative, his point is well taken that God, unable to deliver on the promise of liberation for the people of Israel (hence, the "crisis"), comes up with another plan to save the world. Of course, those faithful to God were simply exchanging the notion of a controlling, omnipotent God for an all-loving, vulnerable God who "lays down one's life for one's friends" as Jesus describes no greater love in John 15:13. God was now not just the God of Israel, but of the world, even the God of their Roman oppressors whom they were thus called to love, even as God made sun shine and rain fall on the just and unjust.

Rembrandt's own subtle reinterpretation of the story of the prodigal, giving the father a feminine as well as a masculine hand, is yet another example of how different ages and cultures freshly interpret God's identity, purpose, and text. We call it poetic license in literature. Among the faithful we could call it spiritual growth.

ᗡᐳ WE LIMIT NOT THE TRUTH OF GOD TO OUR POOR REACH OF MIND,
BY NOTIONS OF OUR DAY AND SECT, CRUDE, PARTIAL AND CONFINED.
NO, LET A NEW AND BETTER HOPE WITHIN OUR HEARTS BE STIRRED:
FOR GOD HATH YET MORE LIGHT AND TRUTH TO BREAK FORTH FROM
[GOD'S] WORD.

(George Rawson, hymnwriter [1807–1889], paraphrasing pastor John Robinson's counsel to Pilgrims to the New World in 1620)

Trusting that all your needs will be
provided for by the One who loves you
unconditionally . . . is trusting that you
do not need to protect your own security
but can give yourself completely
to the service of others.

The Inner Voice of Love, 65

One of the strongest links I have with Henri is that I have
been part of a movement that required me to talk about myself and my personal experience, much as Henri did. I have
had to talk about my sexuality and my spirituality, both of
which are challenging frontiers of intimacy for us all. I have
often felt naked and vulnerable, even when I am alone, away
from public venues. I meet strangers who have an intimate
knowledge of me from reading my books, who "have me at
a disadvantage," an idiomatic phrase we use to mean that
strangers know us in a way we do not know them. And people sometimes recognize me in public places, making me
mindful that my behavior and my words are being observed
critically. My little taste of occasionally being known makes
me realize that those who are celebrities must experience little freedom to be themselves in all circumstances. In certain
circles, Henri was one of those.

No matter how much you give of yourself to other people, I've found, they always want more. Thus there is gossip,
untruths or partial truths spread with innuendo or implica-
tion, sometimes as if they are stark reality. A recent study has
revealed that two-thirds of conversation is gossip: about peo-

ple at work or in the public eye, or about friends, family, and acquaintances.

On occasion, people have reported or asked me about gossip they have heard about me. I found that what had been reported to them was untrue, or taken out of context, or exaggerated to meet the human need to tear down others because of our very human jealousy, resentment, and envy.

Think about the parable of the prodigal son. You probably remember that the prodigal spent his money on prostitutes. And yet that's not what Jesus says. He simply says the prodigal spent it on "dissolute living." It is the resentful, jealous, and envious elder brother who speculates that his younger brother has spent the money on prostitutes.

Jesus himself suffered gossip, as did John the Baptist, as Jesus notes in Luke 7:33–34: "For John the Baptist has come eating no bread and drinking no wine, and you say, 'He has a demon'; the Son of Man has come eating and drinking, and you say, 'Look, a glutton and a drunkard, a friend of tax collectors and sinners!'" Look what people made of the partial truths about Jesus and John!

When you give so much of your own story to others, as Henri did, and as many of us do in ministry and in seeking justice, it is all the more hurtful and offensive to have others take more, twisting private matters into public disregard. Opponents do this; but friends, family, and strangers do this too. That's why it is important to remember who we are, the Beloved child of God, even when we give occasion for gossip. That's also why it's important to remember who others are, Beloved children of God, even when they give occasion for gossip.

ᐁ "THE TRUTH, EVEN THOUGH I CANNOT FEEL IT RIGHT NOW, IS THAT I AM THE BELOVED FROM ALL ETERNITY AND AM HELD SAFE IN AN EVERLASTING EMBRACE." (LIFE OF THE BELOVED, 49)

> We are part of a chain of wounds
> and needs that reach far beyond our
> own memories and aspirations.

The Road to Peace, 11

This posthumous book is a gift from Henri's friend and justice activist John Dear. I'm grateful that this manuscript is now available. When talking about our various book projects, Henri had once told me about an unfinished book on peacemaking that had seemed to him to have passed its time. Not true, as it turns out. Our quote from the book today still speaks strongly to our journey on the road to peace, whether individually or internationally.

Many in the West could not anticipate what would happen when the Soviet Union unraveled. An authoritarian government had held in check centuries-old animosities among peoples who, unshackled, began to fight amongst themselves. We witnessed in horror atrocities unleashed by age-old religious and political divisions. Northern Ireland and the Middle East might have prepared us for generations-old wounding and war, but even in those places and maybe especially in those places, we do not begin to understand the passions and the pathos. And now the West faces religious fanatics of Islam, uncharacteristic of the religion as a whole, who hate us for our influence. And though we react with innocence, like a deer caught in the headlights, our ignorance of their resistance to our far-reaching domination of the world must be overcome and the sources of the resistance better understood. Just as our personal relationships benefit by discerning a loved one's wounds so as not to hurt them there, let alone exploit their vulnerabilities, so international relationships benefit from careful discernment of old wounds and vulnerabilities. Self-interest alone cannot be our guide in any relationship of integrity; rather, our interest should be in that which is mutually beneficial.

But Henri points out that such altruism is difficult to achieve even in our personal relationships. When we are preoccupied with our own wounds, we are less able to recognize that others are wounded as well, especially those who have wounded us. Whatever type of violence caused the wounds— emotional, spiritual, sexual, physical—has its antecedents: violence begets violence. Maybe that's how we can make sense of original sin, or the concept of the sin of parents being visited upon their children generations later. The only thing that stops us from recycling violence is forgiveness. Forgiveness to me is "for giving up" justifiable retribution. Jesus said, "You have heard that it was said, 'An eye for an eye. . . .' But I say to you, . . . if anyone strikes you on the right cheek, turn the other also" (Matthew 5:38–39). Dag Hammarskjöld, who died working for peace as general secretary of the United Nations, put it this way: "Forgiving is forgetting in spite of remembering."

Admittedly, it's hard enough to do this in the personal realm. Even more difficult is to see this as a realistic solution in the political realm. Tending the beam in our own eye, the lack of forgiveness in our personal lives, maybe we can better see to take out the beam (the metaphor of splinter doesn't work here!) in our nation's eye and the world's eye. We must try to forgive our parents, our siblings, our children, as well as our spiritual families, along our road toward peacemaking. Then we may address the wounds of peoples with greater experience and sensitivity.

∾ FORGIVE THEM, FOR THEY KNOW NOT WHAT THEY DO. FORGIVE ME, FOR I KNOW NOT WHAT I DO.

The long painful history of the church
is the history of people ever and again tempted
to choose power over love, control over the
cross, being a leader over being led.
Those who resisted this temptation to the end
and thereby give us hope are the true saints.

In the Name of Jesus, 60

The biblical context of Henri's observation about power ranges from the first sin in the Garden of Eden to Jesus' final temptation in the wilderness. But the experiential context for Henri's discovery was his work with the severely disabled of the L'Arche community. At a mature age, just when he felt the most competent and confident in his own leadership, he learns that love requires a leadership that is not about control but about responsiveness to the actual concerns of those who follow. He realizes that power and control are often substitutes for people who are unable to love intimately.

Even the most powerful leaders of the church today know, in the back of their minds, that if Jesus were visibly present today, he would be challenging Christianity much as he challenged the Judaism of his time. It was this insight that led Fyodor Dostoyevsky to write that exquisite chapter of *The Brothers Karamazov* called "The Grand Inquisitor," in which a leader of the Inquisition questions a heretic whom the reader as well as the Inquisitor himself comes to realize is Jesus himself. Jesus' vulnerability is unthinkable in any human institution. Human institutions are usually organized around power and control, and the church especially, in its claim of divine authority, is prone to this. To believe the church can speak or act infallibly would be heresy to Jesus.

Some who would assent to the church's fallibility nonetheless claim power and control for themselves by appealing to scripture as infallible. This too would be heresy to Jesus, as well as the early Christians, who freely reinterpreted scripture of their own time to suit the purposes of God. For Christians, there is only one infallible Word, and that is Jesus Christ. And there are not enough words to capture the character, the truth, the essence of Jesus, as the Gospel of John attests in its concluding sentence: "But there are also many other things that Jesus did; if every one of them were written down, I suppose that the world itself could not contain the books that would be written" (John 21:25).

Control is, for most of us, the central spiritual issue. Thomas Merton inferred as much in *The Silent Life* when he spoke of our need to overcome the illusion of autonomy. To believe we are in control of our own lives is illusory. Henri even questioned a model I have affirmed in other writings of the Christian's new calling to use power responsibly. For him the old adage is true, that power always corrupts.

What I have found to be true in my own leadership roles, whether in a movement or simply leading a retreat, is that the more I let go of my need for control, the greater the movement or retreat can be for all those involved. This is true in all relationships. That's why Henri couples the temptation to power with a fear of intimacy. When we control others, we can keep them at a distance, a distance that prevents true love. When we objectify others, mutuality is impossible. When we allow others close to our hearts, to the core of our being, intimate connection and community are possible. And we are led even as we lead.

ॐ MAY I TRUST MY BELOVEDNESS, ALLOWING OTHERS TO LOVE ME AND TO LEAD ME.

Dealing with burning issues without
being rooted in a deep personal relationship
with God easily leads to divisiveness because,
before we know it, our sense of self is caught
up in our opinion about a given subject.
But when we are securely rooted in personal
intimacy with the source of life, it will
be possible to remain flexible
without being relativistic . . .

In the Name of Jesus, 32

Moral relativism is the great bugaboo of our time. As an aside
that is not unrelated to my point, I had to look up "bugaboo"
just now to make sure it had no unwanted connotations. I
discovered that a *bugaboo* is a *bugbear* (a term unfamiliar to
me), which is one of two things: a hobgoblin to scare children into behaving, or anything that frightens us unduly.
And that pretty much sums up "moral relativism." The term
is lifted up to scare us needlessly into thinking that it's a bad
thing, that it's the opposite of behaving correctly.

In an era of multiculturalism, we have to expect a certain
moral relativism, what with people from different cultures
perceiving things differently. Did you know that when people view a color spectrum, they will discern at what point on
the spectrum a color emerges differently, given their culture?
That doesn't make one person right and another wrong, just
different.

"Situation ethics" received a similar response when Joseph
Fletcher wrote about the concept in the last century. Situation

ethics was condemned as some kind of moral relativism, when indeed it was merely descriptive, in my view, of how most people make ethical decisions: contextually—that is, within a tradition or culture, and on a case-by-case basis.

Different generations make different applications of traditional moral guidelines. For example, we no longer follow most of the specific applications of the Holiness Code of Leviticus, but, using different applications, many of us nonetheless practice its underlying principles of "holiness": having things or people "set apart" for holy purpose, as well as pursuing "wholeness" in personal integrity and communal harmony.

One has only to look at the church's checkered past to see how differently Jesus' maxims to love God and neighbor have been applied. Today, arguing over different applications of these two laws that Jesus described as pivotal to all moral behavior, we can easily choose power over intimacy, control over compassion. (See yesterday's meditation.) That is, our egotistical need to be right supersedes a willingness to enter into another's experience, and our narcissistic need for control outweighs Jesus' call to compassion: welcoming another's way as a faithful response that may differ from our own faithful response.

Rooted in an intimacy with God, we may know God's grace sufficiently to realize that God's grace is sufficient even if another is wrong, and even if (oh no, it's not possible!) we are wrong.

℘ HELP ME KNOW THE SUFFICIENCY OF YOUR GRACE, O GOD!

The sophisticated arguments of those
who say the issues of war and peace are
too complex for us to understand seduce
us into feelings of uselessness.

The Road to Peace, 4

And that's just what so many "experts" on so many issues
want us to feel: useless, so they can wield their power and influence over us. When I served on a Presbyterian Task Force
to Study Homosexuality, we consulted many experts: biblical
scholars, church historians, theologians, ethicists, and scien-
tists from a variety of fields. Bill Silver, whose candidacy for
ordination as an openly gay man had helped initiate the
study, admonished us not to forget to consult the true experts: gay people themselves!

Having grown up in the United States during the era of
the civil rights movement and the Vietnam War and the Water-
gate scandal, I learned no longer to take the government at its
word. Those experiences perhaps have led to an overscrupu-
losity and sometimes unnecessary cynicism regarding political leaders, but wariness is warranted of all those in power,
thus the existence of check and balance systems employed by
most democracies, and the necessity of a free press.

So when the nation goes to war, the most destructive and
most morally questionable thing a country can do, we must
not allow ourselves to be manipulated by assumed experts.
Traveling through Nicaragua during a period of tense rela-
tions with the United States, our small ecumenical group
learned much from experts: not only the leaders of the Nica-

raguan government, the U.S. embassy, the Roman Catholic
and Protestant churches, but the chance conversations with
an eighty-year-old woman voting in her first free election
and the eight-year-old boy showing us the bullet holes of the
t-shirt he wore, one that had belonged to his brother killed
by the U.S.-backed contras.

And when the nation embraces a "war on drugs" or a
"war on poverty" or a "war on AIDS" or a "war on ignorance,"
we must be careful, first, of such passionate language that
could lead to excess and abuse, and second, of how we con-
duct as well as who conducts such campaigns. Are they leaders who embrace those whom such struggles are intended to
help, or are they leaders who blame the victims themselves
rather than treat them as kinds of experts: the addicted, the
poor, the infected, the uneducated? Just as a vigilant public
and press keep tabs on a literal war, so we must be attentive
to these other struggles, though less sensational.

As the beloved children of God, we tap into an Expert
too frequently ignored in our secular society, an Expert on
values (including justice), on people, on history, on government, on war, on power, and on peace. One does not have to
be parochial or exclusivistic in how one reflects or reveals
such expertise. God's views deserve their time in the marketplace of ideas about government.

ᖇ **STRENGTHEN US TO OFFER THE EXPERTISE WE HAVE, YOURS AND OURS!**

I cannot embrace the world,
but God can.

Genesee Diary, 123

We think too little of our prayer life.

Many of us have wanted to save the world, becoming involved in countless movements for justice or numerous evangelical campaigns. We grow weary, overwhelmed by what needs to be done with too little resources and too few people. Jesus put it this way, "The harvest is plentiful, but the laborers are few" (Matthew 9:37).

In a presentation videotaped in 1994, Henri contrasts the way he liked to do things with the way Jesus did things. He said that, if something needed to be done, he wanted to do it himself. If that didn't work, then he asked people to help him. If that still didn't work, then he decided a little prayer might help. Using the text of Luke 15:12–19, acted out by members of the L'Arche community of Mobile, Alabama, Henri explained that Jesus went about his work in quite the opposite way. First Jesus spent the night in prayer. Then he called his disciples. Then he healed the crowds and spoke to them. Jesus' ordering of things began with prayer, then gathering community, followed by healing and proclamation.

It is only in prayer that we can embrace the world. We are not God. But in communion with God, we can be part of One who is able and willing to embrace the world. We can lift the whole world to God in our prayers, even as we discern where to focus our attention in service. Outside of prayer, according to Henri, we embrace the whole world one person at a time. As a model of this, Henri quotes G. K. Chesterton's description of the compassion of St. Francis:

> What gave him extraordinary personal power was this: that from the Pope to the beggar, from the sultan of Syria in his pavilion to the ragged robbers crawling out of the wood, there was never a man who looked into those brown burning eyes without being certain that Francis Bernadone was really interested in him, in his own inner individual life from the cradle to the grave; that he himself was being valued and taken seriously and not merely added to the spoil of some social policy or the names of some clerical document (*The Genesee Diary*, 133, quoting Gilbert K. Chesterton's *St. Francis of Assisi* [New York: Doubleday Image Books, 1957], 96–97).

We also don't want to "merely [add someone] to the spoil of some social policy or the names of some clerical document," merely fulfilling our social gospel passion or our evangelical concern. But I want to carry Henri's reasoning a step further than he actually does in the presentation. Notice that Jesus provides healing first, then proclaims the nature of the gospel, which, in Luke, is egalitarian, delivered on a level place (as opposed to the mount in Matthew), and justice-oriented, where the poor, the hungry, and the excluded have their needs met (not just the poor "in spirit" as in Matthew). For Jesus in this passage, service precedes proclamation. Instead of our usual proclamation of the gospel in word and deed, Jesus proclaims the gospel in deed and word. This ordering, too, we might take to heart.

∽ YOU'VE GOT THE WHOLE WORLD IN YOUR HANDS! I PRAY FOR THE WHOLE WORLD, BUT I EMBRACE THE WORLD ONE PERSON AT A TIME.

Compassion can never coexist
with judgment because judgment creates the
distance, the distinction, which prevents us
from really being with the other.

The Way of the Heart, 35

This is a tall order. We judge constantly. When we are called
to be compassionate, to welcome another's vulnerability, our
minds are filled with judgmental questions and statements:
Did he bring this on himself? Does she really need to see
this as a loss? There must be another side to this matter. This
doesn't seem very important. Why is she telling me this?
Can't he just "get over it"? No wonder things turned out that
way. If he didn't do this, that would not have happened. And
so on.

What may be worse, our judgments quickly lead to solu-
tions: Here's what to do! This will fix it! Let me take care of
this for you! Don't do that again!

Henri quotes Jesus, "Do not judge, so that you may not
be judged" (Matthew 7:1). My tendency, and perhaps yours, is
to assume this applies to ultimate judgment regarding our
souls, but the context in the teachings of Jesus seems to be
everyday judgment, because of the log in your own eye ver-
sus the speck in the other's eye verse that follows.

In *The Way of the Heart,* Henri tells the story of Abba
Moses, who was asked to sit in judgment of a brother who
had sinned. He tried to resist, and finally filled a leaking jug
with water, carrying it with him to the place of judgment.
When asked about the water leaking behind him, he said,

"My sins run out behind me, and I do not see them, and today I am coming to judge the error of another." The brothers were thus persuaded to forgive the brother.

In Thomas Merton's version of the story, he points out that Abba Moses is black and that he carries a basket full of sand running out its many holes. The point is the same, and Merton uses it to illustrate that in loving another "we have to become, in some sense, the person we love. And this involves a kind of death of our own being, our own self" (Thomas Merton, *The Wisdom of the Desert* [New York: New Directions, 1960], 18–19).

In the book *Compassion* that Henri wrote with colleagues Donald P. McNeill and Douglas A. Morrison, the model for this is God-with-us. And of course we know how God Incarnate entered into our sufferings and alienation and death to bring joy and atonement and life. But all this took place simply by choosing to be with us.

Henri and his colleagues suggest that even or perhaps especially when we feel our presence can make no difference, we need to understand that compassion is not necessarily about usefulness. Just as Henri in other books has pointed out that prayer is often a sacred space and time to feel "useless" in God's presence, so compassion is less about a usefulness that fixes things than about a sacred presence. Beyond the vital import of human presence itself for offering compassion, Christians are additionally "living reminders" of God-with-us.

✵ GOD-WITH-US, HELP ME BE WITH OTHERS AS YOU ARE WITH US.

> My main question became: "Why am I
> alive; why wasn't I found ready to enter into
> the house of God; why was I asked to return
> to a place where love is so ambiguous,
> where peace so hard to experience, and joy
> so deeply hidden in sorrow?"

Beyond the Mirror, 50

Henri was struck by the rearview mirror of a passing van along an icy road he was walking to pursue his duties as pastor to the L'Arche community of Toronto. The driver stopped and took him to a hospital. His spleen was removed and he had lost enough blood to endanger his life. He wanted to make a good death, a death that did not burden anyone with guilt or shadows, and so communicated his love toward everyone, including those with whom he had had conflicts, and celebrated the communion he would have with God. He found himself ready to be with God.

But it was not to be, and Henri survived. Grateful to be alive, he nonetheless felt ambivalent about it, which to me shows both how inwardly dissatisfied he was with life and how certain his faith that "absent from the body, present with the Lord," as the apostle Paul put it. Just as Gustavo Gutierrez had suggested Henri's ministry on behalf of Latin America might be a "reverse mission" in which he took their message back to the influential United States, Henri now viewed himself sent back from eternity, "a witness that speaks back into the world of ambiguities from the place of unconditional love" (*Beyond the Mirror,* 55). Having encountered what in other books he described as the "first love" ("We love because [God] first loved us" [1 John 4:19]) of which all others loves were pale reflections, he wanted to speak from that place to sharpen our reflections — our *imago dei,* if you will.

As Paul wrote in 1 Corinthians 13:12, "For now we see in a mirror, dimly, but then we will see face to face." By means of a mirror, Henri came "face to face" with eternity and realized eternity was here and now. In facing death, he was aware of how dearly beloved he was by God. Having seen God's eternal love, "the glory of the Lord as though reflected in a mirror" (2 Corinthians 3:18), he felt called not only to unbind his wounds one at a time as a wounded healer, but also to unveil God's glory in his own experiences, unlike Moses, whom his people prevailed upon to veil his shining countenance, having been with God.

God's glory for Henri was that "first love." Henri explained in presentations that that's why all others fail us by comparison, because no one can love us as God can. Henri knew from personal experience that the "first love" is an impossible and intimidating standard by which to judge human love. We cannot love, he would say, without hurting one another. He pointed out that those who don't understand their hunger for God's love can become grasping and even violent in their human relationships. Sans violence, he would be the first to say that he knew whereof he spoke.

∽ FILL ME WITH YOUR "FIRST LOVE," O GOD, SO I MAY LOVE OTHERS WITHOUT GRASPING.

It makes no sense to preach
the Gospel, when I have allowed no time
for my own conversion.

The Primacy of the Heart, 4

Recently, during a retreat, someone described himself as a "square peg trying to fit into a round hole," a metaphor with which many participants identified. But one retreatant who worked at a nineteenth-century historical site pointed out something new to us. In constructing a wooden building of that time, he explained, you wouldn't want a round peg in a round hole, because it could expand or contract, depending on temperature and moisture. It was actually better to have a square peg in a round hole to maintain the grip between the pieces.

In trying to fit into monastic life, Henri was a square peg trying to fit into a round hole. He was an extrovert with an introvert's calling. But the monastic life had a grip on him even if it wasn't a complete or comfortable fit. This might also be your experience. Not all of us fit a monastic life, but maybe that's all the better for its firm grip upon us. We are all called to monastic reflection, that is, moments we set aside for contemplation. If we can do this daily, we are all the more blessed.

Retreats are how we are most likely to fit the monastic way of life into our busy lives. It is there we may listen to sacred texts and to one another in new ways, as well as listen to our own hearts, our own centers, and to the God of our hearts. Unprovidentially, many of us want our retreats as full and busy as our everyday lives, and we anticipate a schedule of uplifting, stimulating talks, or we bring many books to read or plan many tasks to accomplish. But we need to find idle time lest we be distracted by time-bound idols.

In a previous book, *Reformation of the Heart,* I described two insights offered by participants in two different Henri Nouwen retreats I led after his death, one at Kirkridge in Pennsylvania and the other at Ghost Ranch in New Mexico. At Kirkridge, a physical therapist explained that a wound has to heal from the inside out. At Ghost Ranch, a ceramic artist told us that, in spinning a pot, the shape of the inside determines the shape of the outside. So it is with the human heart. Our wounded hearts must heal from the inside out. And the gospel we proclaim is shaped by how we allow the good news of God's love to shape our own hearts.

The truth is, however, that healing and love occur in the everyday events of our lives as well as on retreat or in what I call in my workshops "monastic moments," brief opportunities to look inward. Healing and love may come to us in conversations with our friends, in caring for others, in serving a just cause, in catastrophic personal or public events, in life's many interruptions, irritations, distractions, sorrows, and joys. Yet to have ears to hear, eyes to see, and hearts to feel, we need moments of quiet reflection to allow those many ways in which we experience healing and love to consciously convert our hearts so that we may be healers and lovers, better proclaiming the gospel.

൙ **HEAL MY HEART, SO I MAY OFFER HEALING. LOVE MY HEART, SO I MAY LOVE.**

Though the experience of being
the Beloved has never been completely
absent from my life, I never claimed it as my
core truth. . . . Meanwhile, the soft, gentle
voice that speaks in the silence and solitude
of my heart remained unheard or,
at least, unconvincing.

Life of the Beloved, 28–29

In a foreword to Thomas Merton's *Contemplative Prayer,* Douglas Steere quotes William Blake: "We are put on earth for a little space that we may learn to bear the beams of love." Bearing God's beams of love is as much gift as duty: to be truly blessed is a blessing for others. Think of the people you most enjoy being with: aren't they most often people who love themselves as well as others? Loving ourselves and others is possible because God first loves us.

We feel uncomfortable with God's gushing love. An indicator of this is how various translators have dealt with the Beloved Disciple's proximity to Jesus at the Last Supper. Whereas the King James Version had him "leaning on Jesus' bosom," the Revised Standard Version has him more discretely "lying close to the breast of Jesus." The New Revised Standard Version simply places him "reclining next" to Jesus. I have a feeling that the next translation will have the Beloved Disciple in another room entirely!

Tradition holds that "the Beloved Disciple" is the gospel writer John himself, because that is the only gospel where he appears. But some biblical scholars have suggested that the

Beloved Disciple is rather intended to be the reader of the gospel. You and I, then, would be the Beloved Disciple.

But the intimacy Jesus invites of us is too much. Do we really want to be that close to Jesus, for him to know and love us, warts and all?

Blessed Elizabeth of the Trinity, who lived at the turn of the twentieth century, wrote a note to her Mother Superior that was delivered posthumously, challenging her to let herself be loved by Jesus:

> He does not say to you as to Peter: "Do you love me more than these?" Listen to what Jesus tells you: "*Let* yourself be loved more than these. That is, without fearing any obstacle will be a hindrance to it, for I am free to pour out my love on whom I wish. '*Let* yourself be loved more than these' is your vocation. It is in being faithful to it that you will make me happy, for you will magnify the power of my love. This love can rebuild what you have destroyed. Let yourself be loved more than these." (Ronda De Sola Chervin, ed., *Prayers of the Women Mystics* [Ann Arbor, Mich.: Servant Publications, 1992], 201–2).

As we understand letting God love us as our duty, our vocation, it seems less selfish and more necessary. But it is a happy duty. In *Surprised by Joy,* C. S. Lewis recounted how his wife felt God at her heels regarding, she assumed, some undone duty. When she finally gave in and gave her attention, she entered into joy. When we finally give in and give our attention to God, we too will be surprised by joy, and love.

ᘉ **MAY I BEAR THE BEAMS OF YOUR LOVE ON MYSELF AND OTHERS.**

I spent the whole day reading and
rereading *A Rule for a New Brother,* written
by Dr. H. Van der Looy. . . . One sentence that
struck me particularly is this one: "Only what
has turned to love in your life will be
preserved." . . . Loving, then, is the
best preparation for eternal life.

The Primacy of the Heart, 29

What has turned to love in our lives is eternal.

So much of our lives are taken up with things that seem to have little to do with love. Henri saw Jesus' temptations as the three compulsions of our age: to be relevant (turning stones to bread), to be spectacular (throwing himself off the pinnacle of the temple), to be powerful (tempted by the kingdoms of the world). This is true of the overachievers among us, of which Henri was one. If you've gotten this far in this book of meditations, perhaps you are one, too!

But I employ an explanation of the three temptations for overachievers and underachievers alike. Transforming stones to bread is the temptation we have merely to survive at all costs. Throwing oneself from the pinnacle of the temple is the temptation to prove ourselves. Being offered kingdoms is the temptation to always be in control.

Much of our attention is diverted just to surviving: putting food on the table and providing shelter for ourselves and our families. We spend a lot of time proving ourselves: acquiring education and training, working well and diligently, building an impressive résumé. And then comes the time and energy devoted to our need to be in control—of feelings, of time, of others, of circumstances, and so on.

In our workaday world, these temptations may not seem so bad. They may even serve as means to the end of love. But they could become sinful insofar as they throw us off center, "missing the mark," a Christian understanding of sin.

Jesus gives three scriptural responses to these temptations that imply the Hebrew understanding of sin as idolatry: "One does not live by bread alone, but by every word that comes from the mouth of God." "Do not put the Lord your God to the test." "Worship the Lord your God, and serve only [God]." Context is everything. In the context of cultivating the inner voice of love that Jesus heard at his baptism ("You are my beloved, with whom I am well pleased") through a time of fasting and prayer in the wilderness, succumbing to such temptations would have been idolatry.

And so they may become idolatry as we "shape our own wilderness," as Henri described our prayer lives. Anything that distracts us from cultivating the inner voice of love may be a temptation to be shunned.

Yet even in our prayer lives we might be tempted either to over-achieve or merely survive, prove ourselves, and remain in control. "If I have all faith, so as to remove mountains, but do not have love, I am nothing," Paul warns the church at Corinth (1 Corinthians 13:2). "Love never ends" (1 Corinthians 13:8).

Prayer life is a time "set apart" from the world, defended against all worldly temptations. It is a time to bask in the glory of God's love and to love God in return. It is a time to see the glory of God's love for the neighbor, the stranger, the outcast, the enemy—discerning our call to ministry, just as Jesus did.

༄ DELIVER ME FROM TEMPTATION, AND LEAD ME TO SERVE YOUR COMMONWEALTH.

Holding the cup of life means
looking critically at what we are living.
This requires great courage, because
when we start looking, we might be
terrified by what we see.

Can You Drink the Cup? 27

Can You Drink the Cup? written in the last year of Henri's life, takes its premise from the competition of disciples James and John to sit at the right and left hand of Jesus, the places of honor, in his eventual kingdom. He asks them if they can drink the cup he is about to drink, unbeknownst to them referring to his betrayal, suffering, and death. Henri, always writing in three's like a sermon, writes about the spiritual life as holding, lifting, and drinking the cup.

Couching it in his familiar, friendly, homely life as a child in Holland dining with his family, Henri further drains the metaphor by suggesting life as Eucharist, thanksgiving. He speaks of his urbane Uncle Anton holding the first cup of wine, inhaling the aroma, possibly observing hue and sheeting and any impurities. He would hold the bottle, no doubt considering its year, region, and house. From this, young Henri learned that wine was about more than drinking, just as life is about more than living. One must hold the cup, contemplating life's sorrows and joys.

This is one role of the spiritual life, to reflect on the lives we are living. Brother David Stendl-Rast, mentioned in an earlier meditation as having visited my class with Henri, spoke of the Chenchu, a tribe observed in southern India. Upon returning from a food-gathering expedition, the Chenchu would cast a morsel of the food into the bush and offer a prayer: "Our mother, by your kindness we have found. Without it we receive nothing. We offer you many thanks." Brother David parsed the prayer as first, the recognition of a favor received ("By your kindness we have found"), second, the acknowledgment of dependence ("Without it we receive nothing"), and third, the expression of gratitude ("We offer you many thanks").

To hold our cup of life is to recognize what we have received, both good and bad; to acknowledge our dependence on God for life itself and all that life brings us; and to express gratitude for all that we are living.

Prayers of confession in the popular mind are opportunities, corporately or individually, to confess our sins of commission and omission. But confession, in its origin as receiving spiritual direction, was rather an opportunity to stand naked before God, revealing not only imperfections, but strengths; to catch us doing something right as well as to correct us when we steered off course. Holding our cup is an opportunity for confession, "looking critically at what we are living." Yet it is also an opportunity for thanksgiving, receiving our sorrows and joys, as well as our missteps and advances, with equanimity, allowing them to touch and to shape our souls into the persons we want to become. "All things work together for good for those who love God, who are called according to [God's] purpose" (Romans 8:28).

Let us hold the cup, contemplating our life and its meaning.

✧ I HOLD MY CUP, SEEING ITS HUE AND INHALING ITS AROMA, THANKFUL FOR THE LIFE GOD HAS GIVEN ME, PRAYING THAT AGE MAY BRING OUT MY FINEST FLAVORS.

We lift the cup to life, to affirm our life
together and celebrate it as a gift from God. . . .
When we are fully able to embrace our own
lives, we discover that what we claim
we also want to proclaim.

Can You Drink the Cup? 57, 58

Henri writes that, across cultures, people love to lift their glasses in a toast. Some clink their glasses together, others simply look across the rims of their glasses into the eyes of another. But a salute to another or to life or its gifts is always intended. Sometimes my grace at meals takes the form of a toast, especially in public where I resist making a public display of piety, and I lift my glass and say, "Thanks be to God!"

What we are thankful for we wish to proclaim! The most intimate gifts are those we celebrate most publicly, like the gift of an intimate sexual communion celebrated in a church wedding ceremony and officially honored by recognition of the state. Or the sacred gift of a call to serve God's people publicly confirmed in the laying on of hands amidst a liturgy of thanksgiving.

We publicly celebrate young people coming of age or receiving their first Communion. We have parties or dinners to celebrate births and adoptions, birthdays and anniversaries, graduations, promotions, honors, farewells, arrivals, and retirement. All that we claim with joy we want to proclaim.

Yet many people feel uncomfortable and look askance at those who want to claim and proclaim their racial or ethnic heritage, their sexual orientation or gender, their transgender natures, their differently abled selves, their special relationships, their liberation from abuse, and other unique gifts not shared by the majority culture. "Why can't they keep it to themselves?" a person may ask, ironically flashing a wedding ring or proudly wearing their bowling team's t-shirt or displaying a religious bumper sticker. The answer: what's good in our lives we want to lift to bless others.

For my Nouwen retreats, I've created a closing ritual of holding, lifting, and drinking the cup. We pass an empty glass chalice around the room to all participants three times. The first time we simply hold the cup in silence, contemplating our sorrows and joys. The second time we lift the cup in a toasting motion toward others, offering a blessing from our life experience aloud. The words are more meaningful after the prolonged silence of the first passing, and especially after having spent a prolonged time getting to know one another on retreat. The spiritual exercise gives each of us an opportunity to articulate for others something of what we have to offer them, what we have claimed and thus wish to proclaim. (Tomorrow's meditation will consider the final movement of drinking the cup.)

We follow Jesus, who held his cup, contemplating his call in the wilderness and other "lonely places" in prayer, and then lifted his cup in ministry and mission, and drank his cup of passion, passing it on to his disciples who would further his work and take it to the ends of the earth, saying, "Drink from it, all of you." In proclaiming what we claim, we offer one another not only a taste of our lives, but the fruit of our lives, what has grown in our own fertile soil—sometimes, frankly, growing out of life's manure, sometimes growing out of life's more welcome nutrients.

୬ **WHAT I CLAIM IN MY OWN LIFE, I PROCLAIM AS A BLESSING FOR OTHERS.**

Having a drink together is a sign
of friendship, intimacy and peace. . . .
Refusing a drink is avoiding intimacy. . . .
We fulfill life by emptying it.

Can You Drink the Cup? 80, 99

My friend and fellow Nouwen student, Holly Whitcomb, has written a wonderful book, *Feasting with God,* that affirms the necessity of shared meals for spiritual growth of an individual, family, friends, and community. She offers recipes, not only for preparing food, but for bringing people together in meaningful ways. One may recall the concluding meal of the film *Babette's Feast,* in which a French chef creates a meal whose flavors and wines awaken charity, healing longheld enmities among members of an austere religious community. And one may remember Jesus' several allusions to a messianic banquet in the coming commonwealth of God, in which outsiders will become insiders, and all are welcome.

Whether we invite someone for coffee or to rendezvous for a drink, it is an invitation to meet, perhaps to transact some business, but also and often to socialize, to get to know one another on a less formal basis in an informal environment. Accompanying a friend on a business trip to France one spring, I discovered his colleagues preferred to do business over coffee in sidewalk cafes rather than in their offices (to me, a civilized practice!). It can be an invitation to intimacy less available in other settings. If someone regularly declines our invitations, we "get the message" that the person has no time for us or no desire to be with us in that way, for good or not-as-good reasons.

The Last Supper is believed by many scholars to have been one of a series of spiritually meaningful meals that a teacher like Jesus would have had with his chosen circle. It would be a time for offering wisdom and parables, but it would also be a time for cultivating intimacy among the disciples and with Jesus. The trust was so great among them by that time, that Judas's otherwise mysteriously sinister departure was interpreted by the other disciples as his carrying out some charge from Jesus unknown to them (see John 13:21–30). When the thought of betrayal had been put forth by Jesus, the disciples had not pointed the finger at one another but wondered aloud if they themselves would be the culprit (another civilized practice present disciples of Jesus might consider!).

Jesus had already given his life to them. Now he would be giving his life in a new, transcendent way. To seal a covenant in ancient times was to transmute it to an eternal realm. The covenant of Moses was sealed, according to one tradition, with a sacred meal; according to another, through bloody sacrifice. Jesus would be understood to seal it both ways. He would drink the cup; he was willing to die for his friends. But he drank the cup so that new life might be given us, a life of God's eternal love.

In the exercise of holding, lifting, and drinking the cup described in yesterday's meditation, the third movement I invite retreatants to do, one by one, is to tilt the empty cup as if to allow its contents to drain completely into their mouths. I ask them, as they do so, to volunteer what new life they anticipate as they leave the retreat. Frequently they offer some kind of promise, of covenant, to live or love or pray differently. We drink our cups so that new life may emerge.

℘ TRANSFORM THE CUP I DRINK INTO SIGHS AND DREAMS AND LAUGHTER AND CARE.

While Jesus told his followers that they
were intimately related to him as branches
are to a vine, they still needed to be pruned
to bear more fruit (see John 15:1–5).
Pruning means cutting, reshaping, removing
what diminishes vitality.

Turn My Mourning into Dancing, 29

As a writer and editor, I can't help but put the concept of pruning into my own field. Writing is good, but what makes words jump off the page is good editing: pruning, as it were, lifeless, unnecessary words; reshaping phrases, paragraphs, and sections.

Some of Henri's posthumously published words do not jump off the page for me. These are the words that prove repetitious of what he has written in other books, often in better ways. There are reasons some of his manuscripts languished or remained unfinished. Even within his living corpus, there are words like this. But in every book, posthumous or not, there are nuggets of phrasing and insight that do leap off the page. And different readers and different readings give different words vitality, like any good text.

Turn My Mourning into Dancing was first brought to my attention by a participant of a Nouwen retreat I was leading for Oaklands Presbyterian Church in Laurel, Maryland, in the fall of 2001. She explained that, when she had been going through a very difficult period in her life, she went to a bookstore hoping to find a book that would help her. She said that, as she passed shelves of books, a book literally fell off a shelf at her feet! Thus she discovered Henri Nouwen for the first time, and found that *Turn My Mourning into Dancing* met her spiritual needs.

No matter how disciplined we are in our spiritual lives, we must remember the role serendipity and providence play in shaping our own spiritual vineyard. We are not completely in control, nor should we be. Yet both attentiveness and discipline open us to the possibilities of providence and serendipity. The woman described above practiced discipline by going to the bookstore, searching for a book that would help her. Because she was seeking such a book, she was attentive to the book that fell at her feet, picking it up and checking it out. She also had faith that God or the fates would somehow provide.

If she had, in her sadness, sought out a quick fix of alcohol, drugs, food, people, sex, television, or work, she would not have been in a place where a book would drop, seemingly, out of heaven. Spiritual pruning may mean cutting back on all those other "branches" that obscure our spiritual reality: that we are, at heart, spiritual beings that often require "invisible" support.

In the PBS series *The Power of Myth*, Bill Moyers asked Joseph Campbell:

"Have you ever had sympathy for the man who has no invisible means of support?"

"Who has no *in*visible means?" Campbell responded, "Yes, he is the one that evokes compassion, the poor chap. To see him stumbling around when all the waters of life are right there really evokes one's pity" (*The Power of Myth*, 120–21).

Our *visible* means of support are not necessarily bad, but if we rely only on them, we will join the late Peggy Lee in singing with melancholy, "Is that all there is?"

ᖷ **ASK, AND IT WILL BE GIVEN YOU; SEARCH, AND YOU WILL FIND; KNOCK, AND THE DOOR WILL BE OPENED FOR YOU. (MATTHEW 7:7)**

It seemed as if nobody could party
better than these oppressed people.
The flush of victory seemed to have them in
its grasp, combined with the certainty that
they would lose. . . . George Wallace
cannot be converted.

The Road to Peace, 82

Why does racism have such a grip on us? Why do its relent-less talons press into our culture's mind and heart so deep that we hardly recognize its power even now, almost forty years after Henri wrote these words about the march from Selma to Montgomery, Alabama, with Martin Luther King Jr. in 1965? Forty years—we should be at the Promised Land by now. Did our grumbling en route bring us yet another forty years as punishment?

What strikes me as I finally read Henri's previously un-available essays about the Selma march and King's death in 1968 in *The Road to Peace* is the unambivalent clarity with which he describes good and evil, what is just and what is un-just. It's like the realism of his writings about Central and South America: there's a hardness and a leanness to his writ-ing that is less enchanting than gripping. If he had "swung" that way, he would have made a strong politically prophetic figure. Editor John Dear points out that Henri did not want to be arrested in U.S. protests because, in doing so, he risked being deported as an "alien." But I think it was something deeper in his nature that shunned political drama for spiritual drama, the larger playing field in his mind. "Fixing" something politically was important; but addressing it spiritually was even more so. And he realized that "being right" politically did not mean "being right" spiritually; that, as we try to take the beam out of the world's eye we must be watchful of a myriad of splinters in our own, to reverse Jesus' metaphor.

Which brings us back to the talons of racism that grip our culture. At heart it is a spiritual crisis underlying the political crisis. That's why the *Reverend* King could draw Henri from his studies at the Menninger Clinic in Kansas into a march by calling the religious community for support after marchers earlier suffered violence on the Edmund Pettis bridge just outside Selma. Henri wrestled long and hard about whether or not to go, and he didn't so much choose to go as he couldn't bear not to go. That, to me, suggests Henri was not meeting the demands of ego or self-righteousness but meeting the demands of humility and justice. When you'd rather not, but you're there anyway, you know it's not about you.

His recognition that "nobody could party better than these oppressed people" foreshadowed similar experiences with the poor in Latin America and the severely disabled of L'Arche. Feeling momentarily powerful and victorious while facing certain defeat is a dynamic understood by any who have advocated "lost" causes. And yet, ironically, the "defeat" that "George Wallace cannot be converted," is controverted as early as five years later in an essay Henri wrote about Dr. King's assassination, quoting the Alabama governor declaring it "a senseless and useless act." Since then, of course, Wallace asked forgiveness for his support of segregation, probably not unrelated to his own crippling wound in an attempt on his life.

✑ THOUGH [TRUTH'S] PORTION BE THE SCAFFOLD
   AND UPON THE THRONE BE WRONG,
   YET THAT SCAFFOLD SWAYS THE FUTURE . . .
   ("ONCE TO EVERY MAN AND NATION" BY JAMES RUSSELL LOWELL)

If God had not given the gift of song,
this march could never have been nonviolent.

The Road to Peace, 83

Henri's account of his participation in the great civil rights march from Selma is punctuated with songs the marchers sang, both familiar spirituals and new songs for the civil rights movement. He describes not "getting" the melody of one song until a fellow black marcher told him he wasn't "angry enough" to do so.

I have participated in dozens of nonviolent marches and protests that have included a 200,000-strong peace march in San Francisco during the Vietnam era, a hundred or so churchfolk protesting at the Nevada nuclear test site, and a protest about AIDS treatment of two dozen ACT Up! activists. I was thrilled to participate in the twentieth anniversary march of the 1963 March on Washington. But as I read again in Henri's essay of what the nonviolent protestors of the early civil rights era endured in terms of taunts, terror, and violence, my "nonviolence" pales as white as my skin by comparison. Fearful as I was in my own protests, white privilege prevented me from ever knowing the terror that those black protestors and "white niggers," as they were called, endured. I'm not sure I would not have wanted to return violence for violence. And to understand that the nonviolence came from protestors who were already taunted and tortured by a system and society that disregarded and discarded them makes those nonviolent protestors seem like saints who cannot be imitated.

They had their songs, their faith, and their leaders to hold them together. But they also had something stronger: their truth. Even their songs, their faith, and their leaders reminded them of their truth. Singing "We are not afraid" is like whistling in the dark. Singing "We'll walk hand in hand" is hoping against hope. Singing "We shall overcome" is celebrating God's vision before it has been fulfilled.

Their truth was summed up in the signs carried in many protests: "I am a man." The Christian version of such truth would be, "I am God's beloved child." That is the truth that must strengthen each marginalized person and every movement of marginalized people. Affirming it in no way diminishes other people's truth that they, too, are God's beloved children.

Henri was touched by that truth. "I knew that that week had touched my soul far more than one year of study," Henri concluded (*The Road to Peace*, 95). Any who have joined a cause for justice know the truth of Henri's conclusion. There are things that passionate feelings can teach that dispassionate reason can never impart to the human soul. There are things that action on behalf of justice and charity can imbue in our hearts that contemplation by itself cannot.

"Resting in God" is as much about action as it is contemplation. As an old black grandmother said during the Montgomery bus boycott after Rosa Parks refused to give up her seat: "It used to be my soul was tired and my feets rested; now my feet's tired, but my soul is rested" (Coretta Scott King, *My Life with Martin Luther King, Jr.*, 121).

○ **KEEP MY FEET TIRED AND MY SOUL RESTED IN THE CAUSE OF JUSTICE, O GOD!**

"One of us stood up in the middle
of the service and said, 'Ain't you going to
tell us about [Dr. King]? That is why we are
here!' The priest gazed at him somewhat
amazed and said, 'I was not planning on it.
This is just a regular Sunday Mass.'"

The Road to Peace, 100

The death of Martin Luther King Jr. is, for me, one of those rare events of which memory evokes exactly where I was and what I was doing when I heard the news. I had been a mere thirteen years of age when I watched with wide-eyed wonder the 1963 March on Washington, displayed on dozens of television sets in a department store window of a suburban Los Angeles shopping mall. Later I saw the march on the cover of *Life* magazine in our doctor's waiting room, and leafed through the pages of photographs of black and white celebrities gathered for what was reported as the largest rally in history in the nation's capital.

By April of 1968, I was soon to graduate from high school, an education that had transformed me into a progressive liberal. In the kitchen of our small home, my brother told my mom and me that he'd just heard it on the radio. King was not dead, not yet. I remember thinking I should pray for him, which I did. Then came the announcement that he had died. I felt sadness, but also a certain melancholy that I had not followed his work more closely.

Today I live in Atlanta, five minutes from where he is interred next door to Ebenezer Baptist Church and the King Center. I often take out-of-town visitors there at night, when the world is reverently hushed, and the surrounding pool of water reflects the blackness of night. On the rare occasion that a visitor has declined, I have been astonished.

In an essay entitled "Were You There?" taking its title from the spiritual "Were You There When They Crucified My Lord?" Henri explores the initial disconnect from the awful event and the everyday world. He was coming into Chicago from the airport to give a talk on religious development when he learned what happened. The talk went on; people asked questions and he replied; eventually he returned home "feeling like a man who refrains from crying only because there is nobody to receive his tears" (*The Road to Peace*, 99). As with Selma, Henri decided he had to be at the funeral in Atlanta, sitting outside Ebenezer church, then joining King's final march. Huddled on the Morehouse College lawn during the farewell oratory, he concludes, "This was where I wanted to be: hidden, anonymous, surrounded by black people" (*The Road to Peace*, 100).

Before he went, Henri had visited a conscientious objector in prison at Fort Leavenworth, who described fellow inmates' reactions to the assassination, then the impact on him: "I was wondering lately if nonviolence is a real possibility for me. I started to doubt. My friends had been trying to convince me that I was wrong. Revolution seemed the only way. But now I've found my faith again. His death made me believe again." The nineteen-year-old went on to say that, though he and his friends weren't religious, they went to church that Sunday out of respect for Dr. King. "But the priest didn't mention his name," he said, astonished, and gave the above description of someone rising to object.

Henri writes of the encounter with the young man, "these hours . . . seemed more like time spent with a Trappist monk than with a prisoner" (*The Road to Peace*, 100).

❧ "Free at last, free at last, thank God almighty, I'm free at last!" (Inscription on Dr. King's tomb)

"Think of it, think of it! Is there a
better way than to die for garbage collectors?
He died for the poorest, the lowest of this earth.
Think of it! That is what the Lord did."

The Road to Peace, 103

A black Baptist minister who had been jailed with King in
the early days made this observation to Henri while they
both waited in line, vainly hoping to enter Ebenezer Baptist
Church for the martyr's funeral.

I write it here not to begin another reflection on the legacy
of Martin Luther King Jr., but to consider Henri's legacy upon
joining the downwardly mobile, leaving the prestigious cam-
puses of Notre Dame, Yale, and Harvard, first for the poor of
Latin America, then for the mentally and often physically disabled of L'Arche.

I'm sure Dr. King had friends and supporters who urged
him to pick a more "important" battle than that of garbage
collectors in Memphis, Tennessee. Already he was being criticized for distracting from his message and diluting his followers' support by opposing the war in Vietnam.

Henri certainly had friends and supporters who questioned the effectiveness of living with the poor of Peru and
the disabled of Toronto. I've already written of one fellow
professor's rude response to Henri's choice—I daresay the
professor gave voice to countless others too timid to tell
Henri what they really felt about his decisions. But, beyond
the obvious truth that Henri could still reach those more re-
sponsive to his verbal skills and spiritual intellect through

his books, many just didn't understand that Henri did not go to the poor or to the disabled for their sake alone. He did it as well for his own transformation, much like his transformation responding to an interior call to go to Selma or to Atlanta. Just as the prayer life and the monastic life he sought reflected the ancient view of prayer as a place of conversion, so his various ministries reflected the same attitude: these would be places for conversion, for transformation. After all, as already attested, Henri wrote in *Creative Ministry:* "Ministry *is* contemplation."

Today I had lunch with a close friend, Will Smith, who has just arrived in Atlanta to work again with the Open Door Community, a center that provides community as well as shelter for the homeless. Much like L'Arche in principle, volunteers and the homeless form community together. Will believes that, at this stage in his career, recovering the roots of his call to ministry requires this challenging step. Recovering roots is what the word "radical" literally means. In turn, I am challenged by his decision. Perhaps I should be more involved with this community.

Long after his death, Henri continues to challenge readers with his lifestyle choices. And he was just following Jesus' lead, whose own lifestyle choices transform us.

Above my desk hang a picture of Gandhi and a poster of Gandhi's "talisman": "Whenever you are in doubt or when the self becomes too much with you, apply the following test: recall the face of the poorest and weakest man whom you may have seen and ask yourself if the step you contemplate is going to be of any use to him. Will he gain anything by it? Will it restore him to a control over his own life and destiny? Then you will find your doubts and your self melting away."

ᘛ MELT ME, MOLD ME, FILL ME, USE ME. SPIRIT OF THE LIVING GOD,
FALL AFRESH ON ME.
("SPIRIT OF THE LIVING GOD," BY DANIEL IVERSON)

It's nice to know that when
I come back from my trip, there will be
somebody to grab me.

Angels Over the Net, video documentary

Angels Over the Net is a documentary about Henri's love of the
Flying Rodleighs and how he saw their trapeze act as relevant
to the spiritual life, touched on in a previous meditation
based on a passage from *Our Greatest Gift.* As in the earlier
quote, Henri is fascinated with the heroism of the catcher,
without whose vital task the flyer could not do his double or
triple jumps.

But seeing the Rodleighs in the videotape gave me a
more revealing view of Henri's desire. And his casual comment excerpted above gives us an intimate glimpse of that
desire. Though Henri theologizes the catcher as God and our
need to trust in a God who ultimately catches us, there is, in
this quote, an echo of the little Henri who constantly wanted
to be picked up and held as a child. And, though here he is
using "trips" as in flying through the air, still, I can't help but
think that, given his many trips all over the world, there is
something in his words of the yearning of a celibate to come
home to the arms of an intimate companion. And when the
viewer sees the Rodleighs, how fully and how strongly and
how handsomely embodied they are, it does not take much
to leap to the conclusion that a part of Henri's wish was to
be caught by someone as beautiful as they.

Immediately some readers will be offended by my seeming to bring Henri's high-flying theological interpretation of

his feelings "down" to practical erotic desire. But there is no "down" to this interpretation. Henri believed in the incarnation and goes so far as to say in the video that there is "no divine life outside the body." Our erotic impulses, our desire for union with another, whether with another human being or with God, are good and holy and sacred impulses. It is only when we disregard or discard their God-given nature that we fall into error. There is a facet of *imago dei* in us that desires companionship even as it is said of God that human beings were created to meet God's longing. "The body tells a spiritual story," Henri affirms.

In the video, Henri makes the comparison of the Rodleighs being fully embodied just as the disabled people of L'Arche are fully embodied. He had written that Adam, the core member whom he assisted, was bringing him back to his own body. After representing the church, whose spirituality is frequently portrayed and proclaimed as disembodied or even anti-body, and after teaching in academic institutions in which the head is more valued than the heart, L'Arche and the Rodleighs provided a much needed correction to Henri's spirituality. Together they were helping him reclaim his body and his heart. They gave Henri assurance "that when we come back" from it all, we're going to be safe in the arms of those who love us.

Cᴏ Mᴀʏ ᴡᴇ ᴇᴀᴄʜ ʜᴀᴠᴇ ꜱᴏᴍᴇᴏɴᴇ ᴛᴏ ᴄᴀᴛᴄʜ ᴜꜱ ɴᴏᴡ, ᴀɴᴅ ɪɴ ᴛʜᴇ ʟɪꜰᴇ ᴛᴏ ᴄᴏᴍᴇ. Aᴍᴇɴ.

On a deeper level it has given me a sense of my life
as just beginning. . . . I am only 62. . . . The Rodleighs
are saying indirectly to me, "Don't be afraid to fly a little
bit. Don't be afraid to take a few doubles or triples.
If you miss the catcher, you fall in the net, so what's
the big issue? Take a risk and trust.

Angels Over the Net, video documentary

Though he would die two years later, life was "just beginning" for Henri. That's the way it is for spiritually vital people. Life is always just beginning: weariness or wariness or
old ways do not cling. Like artists and children, they experience everything in the world as if for the first time. In another documentary on Henri, *Straight to the Heart,* many as-
sociates comment on his playfully childlike approach to life.
I can testify to it personally, from the big circle dance he led
at a divinity school social to the playfulness he enjoyed with
the core members of L'Arche. Anyone can see it in all the visual documentation of his life.

How old were Abraham and Sarah when they were told by
God to seek another homeland? How old was Sarah when she
gave birth to Isaac? And Hannah and Elizabeth when they
gave birth to Samuel and John? Moses, when he was put in
charge of the exodus? And how old were the temple prophets
Anna and Simeon when they finally beheld salvation in the
infant Jesus? Youth is no prerequisite for God's purposes.

"Henri accomplished more in sixty-four years than I
could in 164 years," Henri's friend Jay Greer says in *Straight
to the Heart.*

Peter, the "rock" on which Christ would found his church, was called metaphorically to take doubles or triples, following Jesus out onto the waves of a stormy sea. Even though the surrounding chaos caused him to panic and begin to sink, Jesus' hand reached out to catch him and help him return to the boat. The faith to risk is all that's asked of us, to have faith that ultimate failure is impossible, because Jesus will catch us, lift us up, into the boat, into God's net.

The Rodleighs, whose name is taken from the leader of the group, would say that Simon Peter lost his concentration. In their act, as in the spiritual life, focus is everything. Two of the trapeze artists learned of their mother's death an hour before a performance. Separately, both let go of it for the time being by dedicating the performance to her in their hearts.

You let go of everything else, Henri says of the spiritual life, to be with God a little. And Rodleigh advises of trapeze artistry, "Do not carry with you the failed trick of yesterday." In developing my prayer life, I learned not to beat myself up if I failed to pray for a day, a week, or even six months. I just began again. Finally it became so naturally a part of my routine, that now I just do it. I may miss a day from time to time, but I don't feel guilty and I return to it.

Henri explained why life was just beginning for him: "As long as you can fully believe in what you're doing at the moment, you can trust it and live in it and enjoy it. . . . The Rodleighs taught me, where you are, try to be there fully. It is in the ability to be totally present *in* the present that creates a glimpse of eternity, of true life, of beauty." Nothing could be truer of the spiritual life. Attentiveness is key.

❧ JESUS, HELP ME TO FULLY BELIEVE IN WHAT I AM DOING IN THIS MOMENT.

Claim the God in you, and let God
speak words of forgiveness, healing, and
reconciliation, words calling to obedience,
radical commitment, and service.

The Inner Voice of Love, 99

Cultivating the spiritual life is not simply to know ourselves as forgiven, healed, and reconciled. We also come to know God as forgiver, healer, and reconciler. At the same time, Jesus invites us to "be perfect" as God is (Matthew 5:48)—in other words, to share in God's identity, who makes the sun to shine on all. In mystical union with God as the Body of Christ knit together in the Spirit's womb, we participate in divine life as we forgive, heal, and reconcile others.

We speak from our belovedness and inheritance as God's children. Claiming the God in us, we can offer forgiveness ("Forgive them for they know not what they do"), healing ("Your faith has made you whole"), and reconciliation ("Love your enemies and pray for those who persecute you").

Spiritual leadership, as Henri rightly interprets our faith tradition, is not based on moral superiority but in mystical interiority. Those who know what it means to be forgiven may unhesitatingly offer forgiveness, as Jesus indicated when he told his proud and judgmental dinner host in Luke 7:47, "But the one to whom little is forgiven, loves little." Leaders who provide healing are those "who can articulate the movements of [their] own inner life," those who "can offer [themselves] as a source of clarification . . . to those who ask for help" (*The Wounded Healer,* 38). And reconciliation is made possible through compassion: "Compassion must become the core and even the nature of authority. . . . The great illusion of leadership is to think that one can be led out of the desert by someone who has never been there" (*The Wounded Healer*, 40, 72).

To the degree we share in God's identity as forgiver, healer, and reconciler, we have not only authority but a responsibility to let God speak to others through us, "calling [them] to obedience, radical commitment, and service"—not to us, but to God. As we ourselves forgive, we have authority to call others to obedience in being forgiving. As we offer healing, we have authority to call others to commit themselves as healers. As we prove reconciling, we have authority to call others into service as peacemakers and justicemakers. Whatever authority we have as Christians comes from God and our identification with God. If this was true for Jesus, it surely is true for his Body, of which we are members.

God often speaks through our actions rather than our words, whether providing forgiveness, healing, or reconciling. Though my brother speaks little of his faith, his compassionate caring for our cousin who struggled with breast cancer, his friend Luis in his dying, our father in his own battle with cancer, our aunt in the frailty of her very old age, and our mother in the years without our father speaks volumes more about God's healing and compassion than all the books I could write in a lifetime.

In word and deed, our belovedness recognizes and greets the belovedness in others, enabling us to forgive, heal, and reconcile as well as to call for obedience, radical commitment, and service to God in our proclamation that the commonwealth of God is at hand.

∞ MAY I BE FORGIVING, HEALING, AND RECONCILING SO THAT OTHERS MAY KNOW AND HEAR YOU THROUGH ME, O GOD.

Thomas Merton in his study about
nonviolence has shown how this taking mode
of existence is based on the concept of the
irreversibility of evil. Your mistakes, failures,
and offenses are unchangeable elements
in the record of your life.

Intimacy, 27

The "taking mode of existence" Henri earlier defines as the form of power that takes advantage and manipulates and objectifies another by his or her "hidden weakness." Madison Avenue and drug dealers use it to sell products. Society uses it to distance itself from ex-offenders, prophets, old people, gay people, people with disabilities, and the poor, to give but a few examples. Governments use it to objectify both criminal and enemy to justify their own use and abuse of power and violence. Churches use it to distance themselves from "the culture." Marginalized groups use it to villainize opponents. And individuals use it to blame or feel superior to others.

The taking form of existence is contrasted with love, which is the forgiving mode of existence. The taking mode gathers its strength around the notion of the "irreversibility of evil," evil that must be destroyed, because it can never be forgotten. The forgiving mode rejects the irreversibility of evil, claiming that it can be forgiven if not forgotten.

Perhaps no one keeps record of mistakes, failures, weaknesses, and offenses as permanent as the one we keep of ourselves. I have discovered that I painfully regret hurts that I've caused others that they don't even remember. I suppose this is better than having an "unquestioned self," how Scott Peck defines evil in *People of the Lie: The Hope for Healing Human Evil.* The unquestioned self is one that fails to reflect on its own propensity for evil. Yet we can objectify ourselves or allow others to do so by failing to forgive ourselves. For example, if mistakes lead me to an attitude that I can't do anything right, then this untruth may become a self-fulfilling prophecy that allows humiliation by myself or others.

Sometimes we internalize what others regard as our "sins," rather than discern for ourselves what are our strengths and what are our weaknesses, or what is sacred and what is sin. This too may lead to our self-objectification, by which we live out the prophecy of others, accepting humiliation at the hands of others as well as ourselves.

God holds us accountable, and then holds us. Time spent with God is a time to be forgiven as well as to be beloved, to let go of our known and unknown sins *for all time* and let God continue to love us as God's child.

Among the quotes taped above my workspace is this relevant one from Dag Hammarskjöld: "Humility is just as much the opposite of self-abasement as it is of self-exaltation. To be humble is not to make comparisons. Secure in its reality, the self is neither better nor worse, bigger nor smaller, than anything else in the universe. It is nothing, yet at the same time one with everything."

ᴄᴡ **BLESS ME WITH THE GIFTS OF DISCERNMENT OF GOOD AND EVIL, DISCIPLINE TO DO GOOD RATHER THAN EVIL, AND DETERMINATION TO FORGIVE EVIL AND OVERCOME IT WITH GOOD.**

> Table and bed are the two places
> of intimacy where love can manifest
> itself in weakness.

Intimacy, 31

The soldier lays down his or her weapon to eat or to sleep. Similarly, Henri writes, love requires disarmament.

The character Huck Finn describes going to church with the feuding Grangerfords and Shepherdsons, and during a much praised sermon "all about brotherly love, and such-like tiresomeness," kept their guns perched handy between their knees or against a wall.

We, too, love love, but keep our weapons handy.

When the apostle Paul wrote to the Corinthians about the proper practice of the Lord's table, he challenged them to lay down their weapon of classism. Apparently they were following the practice of secular dinners in how they partook of this sacred meal: there was a hierarchy of placement of the diners from room to room.

When I became a Presbyterian, the congregation I joined in 1970 had become so divided over the politics of the '60s that liberals sat on the left side of the church and conservatives on the right! We needed to be challenged to lay down our weapons of ideologies.

Jesus sat at table with Simon Peter, someone to whom he had once said, "Get thee behind me, Satan!" and who would deny him later that evening. James and John, who wanted to be first among the disciples and sit at Jesus' right and left hand in his kingdom, were there. In fact, all the disciples had squabbled about who was the greatest. He dipped bread with Judas, who would betray him. Everyone who shared the meal would desert him. And yet Jesus washed their feet and offered them his body and his blood, despite all the weapons of conceit, deceit, denial, and betrayal they brought to the table. Jesus carried no weapon, so he could offer himself totally in love.

Henri describes lovemaking as total disarmament. Yet even here we bring our weapons: our defenses, limited commitment, our "taking mode of existence." Even our genitals, instruments of our deepest physical intimacy, may become weapons, weapons of force or of withholding. But when the nakedness of our flesh embodies the vulnerability and availability of our souls, there is fruitfulness—a birth of relationship and, sometimes, a baby.

On retreats, I occasionally include footwashing. The first time I used this spiritual exercise, a couple married thirty years explained that the intimacy of the exercise was at first intimidating, then profound; another couple who met during the exercise ended up in a passionate relationship. Jesus washed the disciples' feet and, in another instance, allowed his own feet to be washed by a "disreputable" woman's tears. The vulnerability embarrassed Peter in the first case, and the Pharisee in the second.

Offering his body and blood had already proven a scandal to some of his disciples, who left off from following him, scriptures say, when he spoke of giving them his body to eat and his blood to drink (John 6:51–66).

Yet we remember and commemorate footwashing and the Last Supper because they re-present to us Jesus' loving vulnerability, his lovemaking with us, his total disarmament as he embraces the world.

∞ **MAY THE ONLY ARMS WE CARRY BE THE ONES WITH WHICH WE EMBRACE OTHERS.**

We will never be able to really care
if we are not willing to paint and repaint constantly
our self-portrait, not as a morbid self-preoccupation,
but as a service to those who are searching for
some light in the midst of the darkness.

Aging, 95

Henri refers to Rembrandt's painting of sixty-three self-portraits throughout his lifetime, and quotes Horst Gerson's *Rembrandt Paintings* to the effect that the artist was not using his own face simply to save a model's fee but to savor the spiritual within, his inmost self. Like the photographer who makes positives from negatives, an image that Henri later uses in his writings, our self-portraits serve others who follow as a kind of iconography, revealing something of how we have lived our lives, how life and God have touched us.

Henri wrote more than forty self-portraits: his books. Each time he revisited his life, alongside the familiar lines and shapes and colorations there are new wrinkles and textures and hues. The familiar is given greater clarity and certainty and the unfamiliar is freshly sketched. Thomas Merton, in the extraordinary detail of his autobiographical writings, was a Rembrandt of the spirit. Henri Nouwen, in his seemingly slapdash but intense fashion, captured the light of the spirit as did van Gogh.

When preparing for ministry I was required to take several psychological exams. One was filled with choices of how I spent my time. I remember that "reading biographies" was often one of those multiple choices. I seldom marked that choice in my youth; but now, in middle age I would be marking it all the time. I want to know how other people lived their lives and what they learned from living them, or what can be learned from reflecting on them. Sometimes I appreciate the shadowy detail of a Rembrandt; sometimes the illuminating brightness of a van Gogh.

Our interior lives benefit from exposure to spiritual Rembrandts and van Goghs, the saints of ages past whose life details and illuminations inform and enlighten our own spiritual struggles. For our posterity as well as ourselves, it is spiritually vital for us also to find ways of painting our own self-portraits along the way. Perhaps it will be through writing letters, journals, or even books; maybe through recordings of how we interpret a piece of music or literature at different stages of our lives. Or perhaps painting, sculpting, gardening, or architecture may be our conduits for spiritual self-expression. These are intended as mere samples of what we could do, not as an exhaustive list.

Out of fear of self-absorption, we are taught as youths about the fate of Narcissus who fell in love with his own reflected image. But we might look at our faces. How did we earn our wrinkles? What facial features came from our ancestors, and what scars or blemishes came from our own experience? Do we still have a twinkle in our eye? Do we still wonder at ourselves, that God would give us to ourselves?

And we might look at our bodies, our roundness and flatness, sags and firm flesh, color and discolor: remembering how this right arm used to pitch, how these hands knead dough, how our genitals brought us grief or pleasure, how our shoulders bear burdens, and so on.

Reviewing our own self-portrait may give us our inmost selves and how those inmost selves have continuity with the greater scheme of things.

ᐩ THANK YOU FOR MY BODY AND MY FACE, O GOD, THE TEMPLE YOU HAVE GIVEN ME IN WHICH I MAY DELIGHT IN YOUR WORLD AND SHOW FORTH YOUR PRAISE.

When everything is put in its
proper place, there is time to greet
the true reasons for living.

Aging, 77

I've written of a minister facing retirement who told me he
had a little difficulty relating to Jesus because he never had to
face growing old. In our culture, aging is equated with obso-
lescence, and it is this very thing that Henri and his cowriter
Walter J. Gaffney hoped to address in *Aging: The Fulfillment of
Life,* first published in 1976. I did the math: Henri was in his
mid-forties when he wrote this book.

When I did something new in my mid-forties, someone
asked if I was having a mid-life crisis. I was not doing this
new thing out of some sort of crisis. I was doing it out of love.
I left my hometown of Los Angeles to move to Atlanta with
my new partner in life. I was clear about what was important
to me, my "true reasons for living." Thus I was willing to leave
the familiar, my mother and brother and sister, my friends,
and my job. The move was not without fear and uncertainty
and regrets, but the certainty grew with the subsequent years
and the maturing relationship. Even when the relationship
came to an end, I believed I had done what the inner voice
of love had called me to do. I regret having loved and lost,
but I do not regret having loved.

Recent reevaluations of individuals who report a mid-life
crisis have revealed that those same individuals experienced
crises throughout their lives. Others in middle age have arrived at a place of some peace: they know better who they

are, of what they are or are not capable, or what they seek out of life. I know this is my experience. This does not translate into complacency or stagnancy. After all, I still seek—I just am clearer whom and what I seek.

I remember my mother literally or metaphorically rolling her eyes with a knowing smile when I or others mentioned some concern or item of interest as if it were entirely new. Now I sometimes do the same, watching the news or reading the newspaper or listening to younger people. No wonder "the preacher" or better, "leader of an assembly," wrote, "There is nothing new under the sun" (Ecclesiastes 1:9). Yes, there are new "things," sometimes new knowledge, but human interaction, our chief concern, remains basically the same. I have a weird experience of this when I occasionally visit the Yale Divinity School campus. All the students look the same as the students that were there when I was, thirty years earlier!

Jesus was old for his age. (Of course, if you trace him back to the beginning of creation as the Gospel writer John did, that shouldn't be surprising!) Jesus was clearer than most thirty-somethings about what was spiritually vital. Yet the fact that Jesus would press his view to the point of martyrdom does seem like a youthfully passionate thing to do.

But God also worked through old Abraham and Sarah, calling them out of retirement in Ur to discover a new land and start a new nation. And God called the middle-aged Moses, Aaron, and Miriam to lead that nation out of oppression and bondage. So, though life in the spirit may lead to a stabilization of values and awareness of one's own gifts and limits, it nonetheless offers the passion to do a new thing when the opportunity arises, whatever one's age.

ᐭ THANK YOU, GOD, FOR EVERY YEAR THAT I HAVE LIVED. THANK YOU FOR THE YEARS ACCUMULATED IN THE PEOPLE SURROUNDING ME.

Aging can be a growing into the light,
the light which takes away all the dark and
gray lines that divide religious cultures and people
and unites all the colors of the human search
into one all-embracing rainbow.

Aging, 83

Many of us aged considerably in the terrorist attacks of September 11, 2001. We can each point to personal catastrophes that have brought added maturity to our individual perspectives; but this shared catastrophe brought wisdom beyond their years even to the young. In the face of the terrible, partisanship dissipated: between Democrat and Republican, black and white, gay and straight, poor and rich, educated and uneducated, and so on. Citizens and nations rallied around the United States in grief, in loyalty, in an outpouring of support. Even religious division was overcome as Muslim and Christian and Jew alike denounced the religious fanaticism behind the attacks.

We were humbled, but not by the terrorists. We were humbled by recognizing our need for one another. We do not—we cannot—stand alone. It was a moment of history, of *chronos*, marked on chronological time; but it was also a moment of *kairos*, how the Bible refers to spiritual crisis, spiritual opportunity. This terrible experience was a spiritual opportunity to remember that we are all children of God, that we are all Beloved.

Ancient peoples experienced God as "terrible." An encounter with God is also humbling, prompting us to come together, neither Jew nor Greek, male nor female, slave or free, as the apostle Paul said (Galatians 3:28). Categories no longer matter in the blinding flash of the eternal.

Americans and the world have begun to move beyond the tragedies in New York City, Washington, D.C., and the Pennsylvania countryside. Walls and differences and partisanship are already being reconstructed.

The same thing happens to Christians. An encounter with the eternal God transforms us, and we are ready to love everybody. But then we return to building our walls, divisions, and categories.

That's why Henri saw the eternal in old people. Their witness of mutability and mortality remind us all of what a fragile grasp we have on life, how time passes through our fingers like sand in our hands. Many are afraid to be around older people for that reason. Many of these same people will want to visit "Ground Zero" when they are in New York City, yet will hesitate to visit their personal Ground Zero, the place where the eternal consumes our brief lives. Those who are well-aged, who have not retreated as many of us do into prejudice, fear, and resentment, minister to us by reminding us of the light of eternity that shines in our lives even in our youth.

Yesterday I phoned the last surviving family members of my parents' generation, my Aunt Ann and Aunt Grace, 81 and 75, respectively. Toward the end of the call, we laughed about the fact that we spent part of our time over the phone discussing how and where we are to be buried! But in the face of eternal light, even death doesn't seem so terrifying. We belong to one another and to God in death as well as in life.

༒ IN LIFE AND IN DEATH, I BELONG TO YOU, O GOD.

After a long and fruitful life,
one unhappy event, one mistake, one sin,
one failure can be enough to create a lasting
memory of defeat. . . . Sometimes I think
about dying before the great mistake!

Sabbatical Journey, 189

In his June 30 entry to *Sabbatical Journey,* Henri reflects on watching the television broadcast of the defeat of the Czech soccer team competing for the prestigious European Cup. The goalkeeper, who otherwise played an outstanding game, lost the game for the team in the final play of the match. Despite his prowess, he would now be remembered for this one failure. Henri expresses this fear for himself. It is a fear many of us have or have already lived through, some "mistake" that defines our whole life in the view of others, through which they feel entitled to dismiss our many accomplishments or what we have to say. It manifests itself also in the fear that if others really knew us, they wouldn't like us.

I myself have bristled at the way we judge others by a single instance or by a single aspect of their lives. Someone who lies once becomes a liar, someone who is unfaithful once in marriage becomes an adulterer, someone who fails once becomes a failure—all as if one incident could reveal the pattern of their lives. Or we characterize someone by virtue of their gender, race, sexuality, disability, politics, religion, and so forth, as if this one aspect reveals their identity.

Henri died that September, on the very day *The Inner Voice of Love* was released, his journal about an unrequited love. His editors had dissuaded him from revealing the gender of his great love, suggesting such a revelation would interfere with his broader ministry, and modestly labeled it "an interrupted friendship." The wounded healer *par excellence* had come full circle as a professional wounded healer, recognizing the liabilities of vulnerability.

A few years after Henri's death I received an e-mail quoting "the gay theologian" Henri Nouwen. This is precisely what Henri feared, being boxed in by a label that is only a glimpse of his life, not the whole picture. I would never categorize Henri that way. Those of us who have been typecast by one such virtue as our sexual orientation know why some would prefer privacy. Maybe this was the "great mistake" Henri feared.

His *Sabbatical Journey* June 30 entry concludes, "I realize that finally human beings are very fickle in their judgments. God and only God knows us in our essence, loves us well, forgives us fully, and remembers us for who we truly are" (*Sabbatical Journey,* 189).

ᴼᴡ Jesus, remember me—all of me—when you come into your kingdom.

How can I create a friendly space
for the elderly when I do not want to be reminded
of my own historicity and mortality, which make me
just as much a "passer-by" as anybody else?

Aging, 109

Ray Bradbury's novel *Dandelion Wine* follows the summer adventures of neighborhood kids. One chapter describes the neighborhood "time machine," an old person who transports them to an earlier time through storytelling. There are many reasons to grieve one's parents' deaths, but one of mine comes every time I have a question about their past or forget certain details of one of their stories. One of the reasons my parents and I enjoyed one another's company is because I loved to hear stories of the past that they loved to remember and tell.

Old people have not simply traveled through time; they have traveled through space as well. So listening to them extends the boundaries of our known world. We may hear of places we have never been, both geographically and emotionally. They may become our teachers and our mentors, our sages and our guides. At a time when they are misjudged as less useful or productive by contemporary standards, they may be at their most insightful and fertile.

People do not age the same way. Some people become closed, resentful, and negative rather than open, generous, and positive. Some may be open and generous and positive with little or no memory of either the past or the present. Being with such people of whatever age is a challenge, and yet even these can be "read" with care as they drop us clues about who they are and what they have experienced or perhaps endured. Their eyes, mouths, wrinkles, hands, gestures, postures, and clothing speak volumes about their identities. Patience is key to "hearing" their stories, spoken or unspoken, remembered or unremembered.

But we are often impatient, wanting to "fast forward" someone, or stop them from repeating a story, or urging them to get to the point. We may be disturbed or even annoyed by their loss of hearing, vision, energy, or other abilities—especially when they are in denial about their loss, when they resist acknowledging their own frailties. Our level of aggravation may be related to our own fear of being in their shoes, their walkers, their wheelchairs, their rocking chairs.

This is true of any kind of person whose mortality or frailty is evident. We could be them. The person who gave me *Dandelion Wine*, describing it as his favorite book, had AIDS and has since passed on. Persons with AIDS or any life-threatening ailment sometimes endure the same treatment as older people when they lose abilities or strength or memory. Again, "we could be them."

The problem with that way of thinking is that we are failing to recognize that we are already them! We, too, are passersby. We, too, are losing abilities, strength, and memory. We, too, are dying. And they, too, are living. Living with AIDS, living with age, living with life-threatening potential. How we look at it may turn us around, help us to see living where others see only dying, and to see dying where others see only living.

Henri wrote of "befriending death"—that is, becoming familiar with it, making it "family," understanding how finitude reveals the precious quality of life. As we befriend our mutability and mortality, we are better at creating a friendly space for another in transition, as well as ourselves.

❧ DEAR GOD, MAY I WELCOME FELLOW TRANSIENTS, ALIKE AND ALIVE IN OUR DESIRE FOR ATTENTION AND AFFECTION.

The one who can articulate the movements
of [one's] inner life, who can give names to
[one's] varied experiences, need no longer be
a victim of [oneself], but is able slowly and
consistently to remove the obstacles that
prevent the Spirit from entering.

The Wounded Healer, 38

God moved over chaos and called creation into being by
naming it: light, living things, humankind. In the same way,
moving over our own chaos and naming its parts may separate light from darkness, life from death. In ancient times,
knowledge of a name gave power—hence, God's resistance
to revealing God's name at the burning bush. In the same
way, naming what victimizes us empowers us.

Many people stop there. They exercise the power of a
perpetual victim. No one, no thing, no organization, and no
world can ever be good enough to make it up to them for
their victimization. But identifying what has victimized you is
not the goal in the spiritual life, but the means: the means of
opening yourself by removing obstacles to the Spirit's entrance.

Just as we justly urge others to rid themselves of the
racism, sexism, heterosexism, abuse, exploitation, classism,
and so on, that has victimized us, we have to rid ourselves of
the vengeance, the rage, the self-righteousness, the hatred
engendered in us by that victimization. *This is not the responsibility of our victimizers.* They have their own obstacles to the
Spirit to tend to.

We cannot wait for justice or vindication to do this. Most of our struggles for justice and equality are part of a history-long struggle. We will not be fully vindicated in our lifetime. Only having this lifetime to let the Spirit in, then, we need to let go of the obstacles to that Spirit now.

I do not believe that our wounds are obstacles to the Spirit. I believe rather that the Spirit enters through our wounds. We can see and touch others' wounds with tender loving care because of our own sensitivity.

I do believe that our scars and our calluses may become obstacles to the Spirit. These are places where our healing has become ugly or our healing has toughened us; where our healing has turned to unrelenting wrath or hatred (sometimes self-inflicted) or to resistance toward receiving or forgiving another.

The contemplative life gives us an opportunity to assess the damage done to us in our victimization, not so we can ask someone else to kiss it and make it better or demand compensation from victimizers or those who permitted the victimization. We need to take our own inventory and see whether we are returning evil for evil or transforming evil into good—first, within us, second, within our community. There are some among us who are too broken by their victimization to do this, and to criticize them is to blame the victim. But others of us are strong enough to look at the obstacles in our own eyes, in our own woundedness, to the Spirit that transforms evil to good, healing our wounds from the inside out, knitting us together even as God knit us together in our mother's wombs.

☙ **DELIVER ME FROM ALL OBSTACLES TO LIFE IN YOUR SPIRIT, DEAR GOD AND DEAR JESUS!**

Children carry a promise with them,
a hidden treasure that has to be led into the
open through education (e = out; ducere = to lead)
in a hospitable home. It takes much time and
patience to make the little stranger feel at home,
and it is realistic to say that parents have to
learn to love their children.

Reaching Out, 56–57

Both experience and science suggest that there is a parental inclination to nurture and protect offspring. But love is also a matter of choice. Parental love and especially maternal love is likely to want to hold on to the child; but it is the parent's *will* that recognizes when love requires letting go. And it is such love that recognizes and values the child as an independent soul, not an extension of the parental self.

I truly wonder at my parents' extraordinary ability in the midst of life's demands and stresses to make my sister, brother, and me feel "at home," as well as "to lead us out" into our own unique self-expressions. True, stereotypically, my father was more distant and my mother held on more tightly. And, like all people who love each other deeply, we wounded one another in various ways. Yet I am grateful for the comparatively safe environment my parents provided even as they worried about paying bills, the state of the world, as well as what we were up to. I don't mean just safe from abandonment, neglect, or abuse. I mean also safe for us to cultivate identities, embrace values, and pursue goals different from their own.

With similar awe, I have watched my sister raise three sons, largely on her own, and serve as proud matriarch of an extended family that now includes three daughters-in-law and seven grandchildren—all while pursuing two different professions.

In my view, parenting is the most important task an adult may do, yet it is the one for which most receive the least training. To understand parenting as a spiritual movement, as Henri does in *Reaching Out,* is a beginning. He places it in the context of the movement from hostility to hospitality, transforming enemy *(hostis)* to guest *(hospes)*, in this case, stranger to friend. Parents act as hosts and children as guests. A host has not only the right but the responsibility to set the boundaries of a guest in the host's home. We are not to welcome another with an "ambiguous presence," Henri says. We are to be clear about who we are and what are our limits. At the same time, to be good hosts, we are to welcome the guest and the promise or gift inherent in every guest, encouraging the fulfillment of the promise they hold deep within themselves, enabling the development of the gifts every guest brings into the home. As such a movement toward hospitality, then, parenting is as delicate and vital and as fraught with danger as welcoming any guest into one's home.

Just as we learn through experience to become good hosts in relation to other guests, we learn through experience to become good parents, uncles, and aunts. By the time I came along, I believe my parents were more experienced, relaxed, and secure in their avocation than when rearing my older siblings. And grandparents may be the most experienced of all, especially when they grasp that now their own guests, their children, are hosts in their own homes.

☙ HELP ME TO BE A GOOD HOST TO ALL CHILDREN, WELCOMING THEIR PROMISE, ENCOURAGING THEIR GIFTS, REMINDING THEM THEY ARE BELOVED BY GOD.

FEAR OF PRIESTS AND MINISTERS AND CHURCHES

Some people fear priests and ministers;
others feel hostile or bitter toward them; many
simply don't expect much real help from them;
and only very few feel free to knock at their
door without uneasiness.

Reaching Out, 65

Often churches are the cause of the hostility, bitterness, or unease. When I struggled as an adolescent with my sexuality, a minister would have been the last person I would have approached for help because I already felt the church's judgment. Years later, as a campus ministry intern, an anxious student asked me for a counseling referral. Explaining it might take weeks to secure an appointment, I told him I'd be available until then. He declined, saying, "I had enough trouble coming into something called 'The Christian Association,' let alone talking with you—why, you're almost a minister!" And he said that somewhat accusingly. Inquiring further I learned of his negative experiences in his home church.

Like it or not, professional ministers are vested with power in the eyes of others. Serving on staff of a church, I discovered that what I said in committee meetings or even offhandedly in conversation was taken far too seriously. Church coffee hour is a vital time to visit parishioners. One Sunday, greeting someone with a hug, he confessed he had thought I was mad at him because I hadn't greeted him in two Sundays, an unintentional oversight on my part! And recently, leading a retreat, an organizer urged me to wear a nametag I considered unnecessary because of my prominent role, because, he said, "When we come up to speak to you, we get nervous." Anxiety shoots up as some people approach a leader and names get forgotten.

One can see how this form of power can lead to abuse, of which sexual exploitation is only one aspect. Far more pervasive is spiritual abuse, by which a professional minister uses the privilege of preaching, teaching, and counseling to hurt parishioners with ignorance, prejudice, and mishandling of the gospel. But this is not just a problem of the profession. It is a problem with all ministers, all Christians, professional or not. We all serve as "living reminders" of Christ, so we all carry a certain authority with other believers and nonbelievers. When we act out of ignorance or prejudice, or when we mishandle the gospel, the proclamation that everyone is beloved by God, we too engage in spiritual abuse. Have you ever hesitated to tell someone you were a Christian because you feared their negative reaction? I believe that's because we know that Christians are generally not perceived as hospitable. Rather, we are often seen in terms of power and control, seeking another's conversion and conformity—that is, conforming others to our standards.

꙰ HELP ME BREAK THE CYCLE OF SPIRITUAL VIOLENCE BY OFFERING AND
WELCOMING SPIRITUAL VULNERABILITY, EVEN AS JESUS DID.

Just as teachers learn their course material
best during the preparation and ordering of their
ideas for presentation to students, so patients
learn their own story by telling it to a healer
who wants to hear it.

Reaching Out, 67

Patients are people, of course, so what's good for patients is good for people. This syllogism suggests that all of us learn our own stories by telling them to healers who want to hear them. That requires preparing and ordering our ideas and life events for presentation to those who "study" our lives. But those who study our lives are not only "personal" healers, such as therapists. Some who study our lives are "public" healers, such as justice advocates. And still others who study our lives are those whom we mentor.

Writing my first book came more easily not only because it was autobiographical, but because it told a story and stories I had been invited and sometimes required to tell over and over again in my work on a denominational task force, in my ministry, and in pursuit of ordination. I was given a chance to shape and hone the material orally before committing it finally to paper. I had already learned what parts immediately resonated in others' experience—that is, what of my personal experience was universally accessible—and what parts required further elaboration and clarification or plain old cutting. Since the publication of *Uncommon Calling,* the greatest and most frequent compliment I have received from many readers who shared my experience has been, "You have told my story."

But I wrote it also to change Christians' minds and hearts, to transform them into advocates for the full acceptance of gay people in the church and the culture. I have found that on controversial issues, storytelling is the single most effective tool for transforming both ideas and attitudes. I had seen this work in forums my home congregation held every Sunday after worship on the great issues of the time: a judge explaining why he had ordered bussing to desegregate Los Angeles schools, Native Americans objecting to ancestral bones displayed in a local museum, an African American woman who had initiated school desegregation only to change her mind about wanting her child in a largely white school, two gay men who described the founding of the first Metropolitan Community Church in Los Angeles, representatives from the Farm Workers Union detailing the degrading living and working conditions of migrant workers, students explaining their personal pacifism in relation to the Vietnam War. Though we attempted "balance" in presentations of issues, we believed giving such balance required listening first to the people whose stories were being neglected by the media, the government, and the church.

Many people are telling their stories to the media, the government, and the church today. We are learning about more and more kinds of people. Sometimes we are overwhelmed, intimidated, even threatened. But if we recognize each story as yet another fascinating book for us to discover and read, we realize the world is a vast library that can hold as many books as people, though we won't be able to read them all.

And when we join all our stories to God's story—that will be the most complete theology yet!

ᘐ FIRST I MUST BELIEVE IN MY OWN STORY, GOD. THEN MAY I FIND FORMS
OF EXPRESSION TO TELL MY STORY VISUALLY, VERBALLY, OR MUSICALLY.

> Ministers are not individuals who can
> tell you exactly who God is, where good and evil
> are, and how to travel from this world to the next,
> but people whose articulate not-knowing makes them
> free to listen to the voice of God in the words of the
> people, in the events of the day, and in the books
> containing the life experience of men and women
> from other places and other times.
>
> *Reaching Out,* 74–75

This statement may be a little unsettling for some Christians because it contradicts an illusion of authority perpetrated by the church and many of its leaders. They really don't have all the answers. They don't know exactly who God is, they mix up good and evil and miss shades of gray, and they don't know enough about this world, let alone the next. But their income and their reputation and, for a few, their celebrity are based on the pretense that they have the answers.

Often our society gets its religious fix from spiritual "certainty" and "clarity." We sometimes prefer the drive-through window of a religious McDonald's over many courses of carefully nuanced responses to our spiritual appetites in Babette's feast. Fast food rather than fine food. To put it biblically, we are like Esau selling out our birthright for immediately available stew (see Genesis 25:29–34).

Our belovedness requires better answers than what masters of the "quickie" can give us. Finely tuned answers, not one answer fits all. Essentially this is what Jesus said in reference to his teaching on marriage—it wasn't for everybody, he said, and gave the example of eunuchs, nonprocreationists who would be welcomed into the kingdom of God, whose names, according to Isaiah, would be remembered longer than the privileged who enjoyed posterity.

Religious leaders of Jesus' day had the answers too, which is why they didn't like Jesus healing on the sabbath, declaring he was God's child, hanging out with religious outcasts, questioning man's (yes, I do mean *man's*) traditions observed as if they were God's. Sometimes Roman collaborators themselves, they did not like Jesus' conversion of a fellow Roman collaborator like Matthew, the tax collector, into a disciple. We have cultural collaborators today in the United States (in other countries too) who translate nationalism into faithfulness to God and vice versa, who view those who question a national agenda as traitors to God as well as the nation.

These same self-righteous Pharisees condemn those of us who admit we do not have all the answers as wishy-washy liberals, too willing to listen to anybody and everybody (much like Jesus did), too willing to go the extra mile to make sure everyone has shelter and food and health coverage. We are not willing, they claim, to make "the hard judgments," condemning people who are already victims of a system that promotes the arrogant and the wealthy. Many of the privileged distract us with questions of personal morality, whereas the biblical witness (Jesus especially) persistently and most often condemns economic and religious inequities as the most egregious sins. And I mean the privileged in the church as well as society, wealthy not only financially but socially and systemically and religiously—many while being the poorest in Spirit. Little they know of Jesus, and less they would like to know, because the little they know makes them feel guilty enough to want to scapegoat others as "the problem." At heart they fear Jesus is not with them.

ᴄᴡ BLESS US WITH OUTBURSTS OF TRUTH, O GOD, SUCH AS JESUS CLEARING THE TEMPLE. AMEN.

Many people flock to places and persons
who promise intensive experiences of togetherness,
cathartic emotions of exhilaration and sweetness, and
liberating sensations of rapture and ecstasy. In our
desperate need for fulfillment and our restless search
for the experience of divine intimacy, we are all too
prone to construct our own spiritual events.

Reaching Out, 92

The failure of the church to provide spiritual intimacy has
caused many to seek it in alternative life-enhancing worship,
workshops, seminars, and retreats. I guess I part ways a little
from Henri's sentiment in this quote, because I don't see this
as unlike the ancient monastic movement into the Egyptian
desert of the fourth and fifth centuries. We are seeking something the church is failing to offer. The reservation I share
with Henri about such intensive experiences, whether dancing in the spirit in charismatic worship or speaking vulnerably with others on a spiritual retreat, is when they are cut off
or singled out from the whole spiritual enterprise, or when
they cut off or single out an individual or an elite few from
broader spiritual community and service.

A denominational magazine published an opinion piece
on addictions that suggested substituting a prayer life for an
addiction. Beyond oversimplifying a complex human problem, the troubling thing to me about the recommendation is
that a prayer life may itself become an addiction, though not
as troublesome. A monastic who spends all of his or her time
in prayer is also repeatedly seeking an altered state. (A
Buddhist religious studies professor of mine once joked that

Nirvana could be reached by thirty years of meditation or by taking hallucinogenic drugs!) There's a part of me that agrees with Henri that spending time in prayer must be a kind of "useless" time. Yet I also believe that unless the altered state bears fruit, it can foster the primary illusion the monk must conquer, according to Merton—the illusion of autonomy. "Faith apart from works is barren," James 2:20 declares.

"We are not alone. We live in God's world," affirms a creed of the church. The Eden story reminds us we are to tend the world's garden. From the beginning, monastics have been involved in everything from weaving baskets and baking bread to spiritual direction and wide-ranging ministries.

I have led many retreats at Kirkridge in Pennsylvania, and I have visited the community on which it is patterned on Iona, a small island off the western coast of Scotland. Kirkridge's motto, "To picket and to pray," sums up both communities' approaches to monastic life. We cannot tend the world without a spiritual center; but our spiritual center requires us to tend the world.

I know I act better when I have spent time in prayer. I am kinder, friendlier, more attentive to others, partly because I have attended to my own needs. I have remembered who and whose I am, contemplated my own life and story, connected with the vaster picture, contextualizing my life in a meaningful (rather than demeaning) way. Lifting events or people in prayer, I may better attend to the callings implicit in them. God may do something about them through me, as part of Christ's mystical but no less political and physical Body. I am thereby influenced to phone, write, visit, march, contribute, boycott, study, inform, influence, vote, campaign, volunteer, serve. Prayer is not all about me, nor personal fulfillment alone. True prayer is inclusive and is all about *us*, about mutual fulfillment in community.

℘ THY WILL BE DONE, IN MY EARTH AS IT IS IN YOUR HEAVEN, DEAR GOD.

We often see in the center of an
intimate relationship the seeds of violence.
The borders between kissing and biting,
caressing and slapping, hearing and over-
hearing, looking with tenderness and looking
with suspicion are very fragile indeed.

Reaching Out, 84

I first heard these words when I was twenty-two years old.
They clarified the murky passions I discovered in my most
"loving" relationships. Why was it that I wanted to "own" or
"take" the one I loved most deeply? Why should the one who
gave me my greatest joy be the source of my greatest despair?
Why would I wound the very person I most wanted to pleasure? Why distrust the person to whom I entrusted my naked
self? Why back away from the lover who welcomed intimacy?

I realize it wasn't just me. At fifty-two, I can affirm that it's
the complex nature of intimate human relationships. Eros, passionate love, wants us to be one with the other, inseparable and
indivisible. Ego resists. Agape suggests a way of governing our
union: benevolent love. Eros without agape may become heed-
less and reckless, possessive and violent. Eros with agape re-
spects boundaries and mutuality, strengths and vulnerabilities.

This is equally true of making love or building spiritual
community. Both sexuality and spirituality are blessed by the
passion of eros, that desire to merge, and the benevolence of
agape, that wish for another's well-being. The ecumenical
movement benefits from its underlying passion for the merg-
ing of churches; yet the movement is slow because of its ultimate benevolence that seeks harmonious blending—mutu-

ality. As in any courtship, mutuality is developed over time. This is also true of sexuality. Passion may bring us together in the moment; but agape, an intentional love, must keep us together in the long run.

This is true in our courtship with God as well, though, of course, mutuality is never quite to be had with God. Mystical passion may erupt along the course of our relationship with God, and we feel at one with God in the moment. But an intentional love is required to keep God and us together in the long run. The Bible repeatedly witnesses God's steadfast love for us, inviting us to be lovingly faithful to God in return, even during the times we feel the least in communion with our cosmic Lover.

Independently of one another, Henri and I discovered the writings of Etty Hillesum, a young Dutch Jewish woman who kept an intriguing journal during the Nazi occupation of her land. As she approached the possibility of being deported to a concentration camp, her writings grew all the more spiritual, reflections made all the more poignant by her death at Auschwitz. Toward the end of *Lifesigns*, Henri quotes my favorite prayer of hers: "But one thing is becoming increasingly clear to me: that You cannot help us, that we must help You to help ourselves. And that is all that we can manage these days and also all that really matters: that we safeguard the little piece of You, God, in ourselves. And perhaps in others as well" (Etty Hillesum, *An Interrupted Life: The Diaries of Etty Hillesum 1941–43*, 186–87).

Our courtship with the church and with another requires that we safeguard that little piece of God in them. Our courtship with God requires that we safeguard that little piece of God in ourselves.

ॐ You CANNOT PROMISE US SAFETY IN THIS WORLD, BUT YOU PROMISE US SAFETY IN YOUR LOVE. I PROMISE YOU SAFETY IN MY HEART: THERE WILL ALWAYS BE A SANCTUARY WITHIN ME FOR YOUR HOLY PRESENCE, O GOD.

My own heart seems like a microcosm
of the world of violence and destruction in which I
live. I have not killed with my hands, but how well
do I know the sentiments of my heart . . . ?

Heart Speaks to Heart, 40

The origin of *Heart Speaks to Heart* is as vital a story as
the product. Henri found value in meditating on a Robert
Lentz icon he had commissioned of the beloved disciple
John leaning against Jesus' breast in the heavenly Jerusalem.
Entitled, "The Bridegroom," it evoked in Henri his hunger to
be close to the heart of Jesus. He sent copies to many friends,
including me. But it was the one he framed for "Mammy"
Vanier, L'Arche founder Jean Vanier's eighty-seven-year-old
mother, that prompted her persistent efforts to persuade
Henri to write about the Sacred Heart of Jesus, an object of
piety in the nineteenth century.

It made me think of the framed picture of Jesus on velvet
that hung in my grandmother's home in Kansas, undoubtedly
a gift from the kindly nuns who cared for her during her frequent hospitalizations at Mt. Carmel, a Roman Catholic hospital in her small town of Pittsburg. At its center was the
Sacred Heart surrounded and wounded by a crown of thorns.
For me, a young Baptist boy from California, it seemed a dark
image from a religious past. Thus I could understand Henri's
reluctance to write about the Sacred Heart.

When Henri's own heart was broken by unrequited love
and he took an extended period away from his community to
heal, he spent Holy Week in a Trappist monastery in Holland,

Manitoba. There he realized that, on Holy Thursday, Good Friday, and Easter Sunday, instead of writing *about* the Sacred Heart of Jesus, he wanted to write prayers *to* that Sacred Heart. Today's excerpt is taken from his prayer written on Good Friday.

What it reveals is the inevitable result of intimacy with Jesus, with God, as Brother Thomas Keating has written of it: our shadow side emerges in the light of God's presence, those thoughts and feelings we suppress in our desire to serve God and serve others, to be loving and good and holy. We like to hold ourselves above those who crusaded against Muslim "infidels," above those who tortured Jews and other "heretics" in the Inquisition, above those who perpetrated the *shoah* (or holocaust) against Jews, Romas (gypsies), gays, religious minorities, and political dissidents, above those who enslaved Africans or who racially discriminate, above those who treated women as chattel or second-class citizens, above those who bash homosexuals. But as the light of Jesus darts around inside our hearts, we discover similar shadows lurking in corners, a holocaust waiting for its time when we are tired, stressed, angry, resentful. We may only kill in our hearts, but, as Jesus testified, what we conceive is hurtful too.

Like the demons backed into corners of the hearts of those they convulsed in Jesus' presence, so these hide until an opportune time, as Jesus' tempter in the wilderness, returning later with greater force as the "seven other spirits more evil" join an outcast "unclean spirit," despite the person's housecleaning (Luke 11:24–26).

Saints are those who are not demon-free, but aware of their own demons, their own shadows. Intimacy with Jesus allows them to see the difference between his divinity and theirs.

ॐ **THOUGH I WALK THROUGH A VALLEY OF SHADOWS, I FEAR NO EVIL, FOR YOU ARE WITH ME.**

> How can all of my life be Eucharistic . . . ?
> I have to come up with my own response.
> Without such a response, the Eucharist may
> become little more than a beautiful tradition.

With Burning Hearts, 12

"I have to come up with my own response" must be our own conclusion. We must find ways for the Eucharist to be incorporated into our everyday lives, else it will seem only otherworldly and magical rather than this-worldly and practical. By this I don't mean we should in any way diminish its sacred glow; rather, I mean we should bring out the sheen of everyday life.

During a public talk, Henri concluded that life is a brief time for us, as God's beloved children, to say to God, "I love you, too." From the perspective of the Eucharist, he concludes that "the Eucharistic life" is "the life in which everything becomes a way of saying 'Thank you'" to God (*With Burning Hearts,* 95).

I mentioned a divinity school course that Henri audited. It was entitled "Emotions, Passions, and Feelings." I wrote a short story for the class about a young woman who discovers within herself the capability to "be" grateful without always "feeling" gratitude—the distinction between choosing to cultivate an attitude of gratitude rather than simply relying on unchosen and unpredictable feelings. As she developed the attitude, however, the feelings of gratitude came more frequently. The fictional story reflected what we were learning: that our wills play an enormous role in how we experience life. I had always been taken with the concept of "the will to believe," that faith does not necessarily come "naturally," but may be the product of our willing desire to believe. In *The Varieties of Religious Experience*, William James had written that "overbeliefs," that is, beliefs for which we have little or no empirical evidence, can give birth to realities. For example, if we anticipate someone to be friendly or unfriendly, our approach might elicit the expected response. If we view life as a gift, everything may be an occasion for gratitude. If we view life as sacred, we come to view life's events as sacramental. "The movement from resentment to gratitude, that is, from a hardened heart to a grateful heart" (*With Burning Hearts*, 13) is necessary to live a Eucharistic life, a life of thanksgiving (the meaning of Eucharist).

"You have been staring at an obstacle not willing to consider that the obstacle was put there to show you the right path" (*With Burning Hearts*, 42). What prevents this attitude toward life from becoming syrupy sweet, overly sentimental? A librarian once shocked me by declaring that, as a child, she had burned *Pollyanna* in disgust! For Henri, true gratitude requires first "mourning our losses," allowing ourselves to grieve that life doesn't always turn out as planned. Only then can we honestly and unsentimentally embrace the obstacles, the bad breaks, the tragedies, even the bad people as occasions for new life, new directions, new opportunities.

In St. Louis, a laywoman I'd known surprised me by appearing in a clerical collar. When I asked how this came to be, she described two horrific events: one of being mugged, another of being raped. Within these wounds, she heard a call to the Episcopal priesthood. No doubt disgust, shame, grief, and rage came first; but what came next was religious vocation. It was like meeting in real life the woman of whom I had written!

ᏅᎳ **May I find gratitude in my heart for all of my life today. As I "re-member" the past, may I mourn my losses while embracing my gains in thanksgiving.**

But as we grow older we discover that
what supported us for so many years—prayer,
worship, sacraments, community life, and a
clear knowledge of God's guiding love—
has lost its grip on us.

With Burning Hearts, 26

Henri notes the Eucharist begins with "Lord, have mercy."
He interprets the cry for mercy more broadly than asking
forgiveness for sins. In a sense, it is almost inviting our forgiveness of God, because it is the movement by which we
grieve our losses, all that comes between us and God. Our
sins, yes, but others' sins and systemic sin and the absence of
God's intervention on our behalf. The prayer of confession
may become a prayer for deliverance. We can overcome the
fact that "long-cherished ideas, long-practiced disciplines,
and long-held customs of celebrating life can no longer
warm our hearts" by allowing "tears of our grief . . . [to] soften
our hardened hearts and open us to the possibility to say
'thanks'" (*With Burning Hearts,* 26, 30).

Marcus Borg, in his book *Meeting Jesus Again for the First
Time,* delineates three "macro" stories in the Bible: 1) exodus
from oppression to a promised land; 2) exile from our spiritual center and our return; and 3) sin and alienation and
atonement. Borg laments that the latter story has captured
the spiritual imagination of the church to the detriment of
the first two, as we reenact our alienation and Christ's atonement in Sunday liturgies. The first two have power because
they involve movement from here to there, from Egypt to the
Promised Land, from Jerusalem to the far reaches of the

Babylonian Empire and home again. But the priestly story of atonement serves as a repetitive cycle fostering a passive spiritual community, losing its grip on us as a summer rerun.

Researching my book *Coming Out As Sacrament,* I learned that sacrifices were not intended to placate an angry God but to purify the spiritual community so they might continue to enjoy God's holy presence. Sacrifices, then, were about maintaining the status quo rather than forward movement.

I believe we "can have it all," all three stories re-presented, reenacted during the Eucharist. The Last Supper parallels the Passover Seder, wherein the liberating act of God, the Exodus, is remembered: a meal of bread we've not taken the time to leaven because we're in a hurry to leave for the Promised Land. Our "Lord, have mercy" could become a prayer for liberation from all within us and our culture and church that holds us in bondage, that keeps us from moving forward to the messianic banquet of the inbreaking commonwealth of God.

And, just as the Israelites were exiled from their spiritual center of Jerusalem, home of the Temple, the same worldly forces deprive us of our spiritual center, Jesus Christ, our new temple, destroyed in crucifixion and yet raised again for us, a spiritual center who does not stay in Jerusalem but goes to the furthest parts of the world to welcome exiles home as "members of the household of God" (Ephesians 2:19). We ourselves are called out as living stones built into a spiritual house to be a holy priesthood (1 Peter 2:5).

When we allow all three macrostories of scripture to blend in the Eucharist, there is a lot more movement than meets the eye. No longer "only" a sacrament of at-one-ment between Creator and creature, it serves as a sacrament of liberation, journey, and destiny, as well as a sacrament of exile and homecoming.

ᕴ **MOVE ME! MAKE MY HEART BURN FOR MOVEMENT FROM THE WAYS THINGS HAVE BEEN TO THE WAY THINGS SHOULD BE.**

It is one of the characteristics of our
contemporary society that encounters, good as
they may be, don't become relationships. . . .
Jesus is a very interesting person . . . But do
we want to invite him into our home?

With Burning Hearts, 56–57

Even in the Christian circles in which I move, people do not talk very much about Jesus. In our multicultural society, it's as if we're embarrassed to think or say or believe that a male Jew of first century Palestine is vital to our spirituality. We have less problem with Buddhists contemplating Buddha or Muslims revering Mohammed. Many Christians refer to "Christ" or the "Christ-event" rather than Jesus to make some sort of ideologically sanitary distinction that I don't quite get. Buddhists are called to be Buddhas, but Christians are not called to be Christs, just Christ's.

I was invited to preach for a newly formed congregation in Kalamazoo, Michigan, that was to vote shortly before my visit on whether to affiliate with the Unitarian Universalist Association or with the United Church of Christ. I urged them to let me know their decision as soon as possible after their vote, so I might prepare an appropriate sermon. When they affiliated with the UCC, I gave a sermon about Jesus, using John 6, about Jesus offering his body and blood to his disciples, an image that alienated some disciples even then. I admit that I have concerns about the way the Gospel writer John depicts Jesus as so self-confident as to sound arrogant. Though nervous about talking about Jesus in what appeared to be a rigidly progressive congregation, I thought I'd done a good job with the text as metaphor to affirm an embodied spirituality needed for spiritually based justice efforts. But the talk-back session following the worship was filled with anger at "exclusivistic" claims about Jesus.

As one who uses spiritual resources from many faiths and other sources in my own morning prayers, I hardly think of Jesus as the only way to God. But I do affirm that, more than anyone for me, he "got it right" spiritually. That's why I'm a follower of Jesus. That's why I can say, "I believe . . . ," a confession of faith. "And *faith*, as the Greek word *pistis* shows, is an act of trust," Henri writes of the creed that comes between the proclamation of the word and the distribution of the Eucharistic gifts (*With Burning Hearts*, 59). Trust is required to invite anyone into our home, including Jesus.

Henri illustrates how many interesting people each of us encounters in our work, travel, social occasions, and so forth. He implies that a lack of trust in our contemporary society prevents us from inviting them over, welcoming them into our houses. Extrovert that he was, he overlooks that our contemporary society puts us in contact with hundreds more people than our ancestors. The question is not just about trust, but about commitment of our time and resources.

Similarly, it's not only about trusting intimacy with Jesus, but about commitment of our time and resources to him. Henri writes about the travelers to Emmaus who encounter, at first unaware, the risen Jesus: "The two disciples who trusted the stranger enough to let him enter into their inner space are now led into the inner life of their host" (*With Burning Hearts*, 65).

During a Eucharist, a church friend passed the elements without receiving. I was deeply impressed when he explained that he believed in Jesus, but did not want to receive Holy Communion until he was ready to fully commit himself to him.

ᘒ **MAY I BE RECEPTIVE TO YOU, JESUS, EVEN AS I RECEIVE YOU, THE HOST.**

Celebrating the Eucharist requires
that we stand in this world accepting
our co-responsibility for the evil that
surrounds and pervades us.

With Burning Hearts, 32

Recently, leading a committee, I offered a *mea culpa* for a mistake I had made. A member of the committee cheered me enormously when he smiled incredulously and said, "Most people would try to excuse their mistake or try to blame others. It's outstanding that you own your mistake." His comment made me feel so good I wanted to confess other mistakes, even if I had to make them up!

Afterward I thought what a different world we would have if we all felt secure enough with others to confess mistakes without being labeled, ridiculed, or made to suffer. My security in this case lay in the fact that I knew the committee members loved me and would forgive me for my error. Contrasting this to our experience of much spiritual community makes me realize how far we fall short of being a truly loving community.

When we are attacked, it is much more difficult to admit that we are wrong. I was passionately angry with those who tried to lay the blame of the September 11, 2001, terrorist attacks on the United States for our policies in the Middle East, even though I don't agree with those policies. To me it was another case of "blaming the victim," something most people would resist doing if it involved a victim of any other form of violence, such as rape, domestic abuse, or street bashing.

However, having said that and still believing it, I nonetheless realize the basis for my angry defensiveness. The United States had not first been allowed by critics to "mourn our losses" before being required to re-view ourselves and our relationship with the world.

The corporate prayer of confession or prayer for deliverance is an opportunity to mourn our losses together. I remember in the '60s and the '70s when fellow church members objected to confessing society's sins as their own, saying things like: "I'm not responsible for racial discrimination." "I'm not responsible for the nuclear threat." "I'm not responsible for the war in Vietnam." And yet, as Martin Luther King Jr. said, if we're not part of the solution, we're part of the problem. Inertia is the greatest contributor to injustice. Inertia is "a property of matter by which it continues in its existing state of rest or uniform motion in a straight line, unless that state is changed by an external force." Inertia is one of the seven deadly sins: sloth. If we don't play a part in shifting society's (or the church's) direction, then we share responsibility for its misdirection.

As the United States and other nations who lost citizens in the attacks mourn our losses over the September 11 terrorist attacks, we must "stand in this world accepting our coresponsibility," *never* for those horrific acts of violence, but for inequities between East and West, among Jew and Christian and Muslim.

For Christians, such a *mea culpa* enables us to be receptive to the ultimate victim of terrorism, Jesus Christ. In the presence of his own forgiving love, we may feel secure and happy to confess mistakes.

ᐁ LORD, I AM NOT WORTHY TO RECEIVE YOU. ONLY SAY THE WORD, AND I SHALL BE HEALED.

Precisely because the table is the
place of intimacy for all the members
of the household, it is also the place
where the absence of that intimacy is
most painfully revealed.

With Burning Hearts, 60

The most rewarding course I took at Yale Divinity School was
the seminar Henri led on the life and ministry of Vincent van
Gogh my final semester. "Didn't he kill himself?" his academic
colleagues questioned when Henri first suggested the class.
"What ministry?" We learned that van Gogh began as a
Calvinist minister to the coal miners of the Borinage, where he
scandalized church officials by living like the poor miners,
going down into the mines, giving them his possessions, including his bed to a sick woman. He was removed by the
church, and after an intentional, idle period—his wilderness—
discerned that his ministry would be painting, hoping his
paintings would have "the same consoling effect" that the
church used to have. I identified with van Gogh's inability to "fit
in" within the church, his ardent passion and compassion for
people, as well as the artist within yearning to come out. My art
was writing rather than painting, and my final paper for the
class was a story about a young woman ministered to by two of
his paintings, the most fulfilling writing I did in divinity school.

Henri felt an affinity with this artist from his homeland
for many of the same reasons. Vincent painted peasants, ordinary people doing ordinary things, yet his paintings had
the sacred vividness of stained glass windows. "I like so

much better to paint the eyes of people than to paint cathe-drals," he wrote his brother and patron Theo. Vincent's cor-respondence to Theo (which you cannot miss means "God") was our primary written text. Vincent's paintings, of course, were our primary visual texts.

Perhaps no painting of Vincent's depicts the noticeable absence of intimacy around the table of which Henri writes than Vincent's *The Potato-Eaters*. I first saw it as a reproduc-tion and later in the van Gogh museum in Amsterdam. It is a dark and brooding portrait of a peasant family eating pota-toes and drinking coffee, lit by a single lantern hung from the ceiling. Their faces are as craggy and earthen as the potatoes they eat. Of the five figures, none is making eye contact and none appears to be smiling. A matronly woman is looking down at the coffee she is pouring, an older man is looking at her as he holds up his cup, a young woman is looking at the young man next to her at table, who seems lost in thought, maybe looking toward the older woman. The silhouette of a child is centered between the pairs, her back to the artist. No one is looking at her, and the tilt of her head suggests to me she's gazing at the potatoes. Family members seem isolated from one another, loneliness apparent in a few of their faces.

This is life, and this is life in the church. As we gather around our tables, as family or as spiritual family, it becomes clear whether we are blessed with intimacy or cursed with its absence. Paul warned Corinthians gathering around Christ's table that those "who eat and drink without discerning the body, eat and drink judgment against themselves" (1 Corinthi-ans 11:29). The context suggests that we come under judgment as a church when we fail to recognize our spiritual intimacy with one another. Christ calls us to his table not just to give thanks, but to remind us of our kinship.

∾ INTOXICATE US WITH THE INTIMACY OF THE NEW COVENANT COMMUNITY AS WE FEED ON YOU IN OUR HEARTS.

RECEIVING FROM THOSE TO WHOM WE ARE SENT

> It is so easy to narrow Jesus down to our Jesus,
> to our experience of his love, to our way of knowing
> him. . . . But we will soon be burned out if we
> cannot receive the Spirit of the Lord from those
> to whom we are sent.

With Burning Hearts, 85, 89

Henri concludes this meditation on the Eucharist with the final charge from the mass, "Ite Missa est," "Go, this is your mission." The way he puts it in *Can You Drink the Cup?* is that what we claim we also want to proclaim. We naturally want to proclaim however we "claim" Jesus. Yet Jesus is not ours to claim alone. In the Eucharist, each one of us receives only a small taste. To get full-bodied flavor, as well as have enough to be satisfied, we listen in scripture, in worship, in community, and in ministry to how others experience Jesus in their lives. And just as the travelers to Emmaus returned to tell fellow disciples in Jerusalem how they recognized Jesus at their table, we are called to tell others how and where we see his Spirit today.

We are not just sent to one another: "We are sent to the sick, the dying, the handicapped, the prisoners, and the refugees to bring them the good news of the Lord's resurrection" (*With Burning Hearts*, 89). In his wide-ranging ministry, Henri took this literally, not only ministering to the listed categories, but adding many more new ones, some quite untraditional. For example, Henri served the poor, but he also served the rich, cultivating their philanthropy. All were represented in his three-hour "farewell" at the unfinished Slavic-style Cathedral of the Transfiguration, replete with golden onion domes rising above Richmond Hill, Ontario. In life and in death, Henri was in the vestibule of an incomplete church, welcoming others and their own experiences of God. "We will soon be burned out if we cannot receive the Spirit of the Lord from those to whom we are sent," is the sentence that follows the list of those to whom we proclaim the resurrection (*With Burning Hearts*, 89).

In *Creative Ministry*, Henri tells the story of himself as a young priest visiting a family whose children slept several to a bed. He decided that what they needed were additional beds, so he purchased beds for them. On his next visit he found the family had sold the beds so they could give a party for all of their friends. He realized that what they needed was the party, not the beds, as he had imagined. "When only one gives and the other receives, the giver will soon become an oppressor and the receivers, victims," Henri asserts (*With Burning Hearts*, 89). In other words, our gifts may become a subtle means of manipulation. But what the family taught Henri was their need—and his need—for celebration over comfort.

When we proclaim Jesus in word and deed, we give him to others. He is no longer just "ours." He is "theirs" as well. As they recognize him in the world and return to tell us, we must listen to know Christ more fully and to keep our hearts full. Though Jesus began as a young Palestinian Jewish male in the first century, now the Body of Christ is male and female, of every race and culture, of varying abilities and orientations and ages, of every time and place, in this life and the life beyond. We must let this expansive Body of Christ breathe on us the Spirit as Jesus breathed on his disciples, saying, "Receive the Holy Spirit" (John 20:22).

∾ BREATHE ON ME, BREATH OF GOD,
  FILL ME WITH LIFE ANEW,
  THAT I MAY LOVE WHAT THOU DOST LOVE,
  AND DO WHAT THOU WOULDST DO.
  ("BREATHE ON ME, BREATH OF GOD" BY EDWIN HATCH)

> The really great saints of history
> don't ask for imitation. Their way was unique
> and cannot be repeated. But they invite
> us into their lives and offer a hospitable
> space for our own search.
>
> *Reaching Out,* 100

Few things aggravate me more than when someone declares, for example, that Martin Luther King Jr. wasn't a "saint" because of allegations about his private life or academic work. Or another person questions the sainthood of Mother Teresa because she failed to address problems systemically and politically. Saints are not perfect people. Saints can't and don't do everything. Saints are people who do the right thing and move people to do the right thing. Ultimately, I don't believe God cares so much about moral perfection or ideological correctness. I believe God values compassion.

Henri went out of his way to confess his weaknesses, failures, and mistakes. That he kept a part of himself hidden should not diminish that he revealed so much. That he was not as literary and scholarly as a Thomas Merton or Simone Weil nor as political as a Daniel Berrigan or Dorothy Day does not take away from his gifts of awakening us to the spiritual life. That he was frenetic and driven only sets in clear relief his seeking a spiritual center of calm. That he was lonely and hungry for intimacy unveils what I believe to be the mystery of God's own self, seeking companionship by creating a world, becoming one of us, and now giving the divine Spirit to live in our hearts.

Henri wanted to pray and invited us to pray. What greater gift could he offer? He embodied, as saints tend to do, the spiritual hunger and thirst of his era. Though he eschewed relevancy as one of the compulsions of our time, he was nonetheless quite relevant, quite necessary as a corrective to our demythologized, deconstructed world. He recognized that science and religion—in his case, psychology and faith—found their integrity in the spiritual life. The spiritual life is both a quest for truth and a trust that there is truth. Saints offer us their challenge of quest and their faith in truth.

You will remember the earlier description of the video *Angels Over the Net,* in which Henri is enthralled with the trapeze artists, the Flying Rodleighs. He feels as if his life is just beginning, though he would die a short two years later. He is more aware than ever that, in being attentive to the "now," one glimpses the eternal. He again describes the catcher, not the flyer, as the real hero. He talks about how, at the end of the day, we want a catcher, someone who, after we do our double and triple flips, grabs us and holds us and welcomes us home. At the end of his days, Henri had faith that the Divine Catcher would do just that.

But as he is lifted above the canopy of the circus tent, he tosses us his mantle, his forty-plus books on the spiritual life, in the hopes that we, too, will join the circus and do doubles and triples as the glory of God, the Beloved, not worrying about the mistakes of yesterday, keeping faith in the strength and love of the Catcher, who will lift us up, and carry us home.

ᑫᐧ LIFT US UP AND CARRY US HOME!

ACKNOWLEDGMENTS

✳

Before I wrote the one-hundredth and final meditation of this book on an early Sunday evening, I took down the clear glass chalice I use for my Henri Nouwen retreats and workshops and filled it with wine. I did so in thanksgiving, in thanksgiving to God for so many. For Jesus, who started it all. For Henri, responsible for so much of my spiritual formation. For Sue Mosteller, Henri's literary executrix, and Wendy Lywood, an Anglican priest, both from Daybreak, the L'Arche community of Toronto, with whom I have led retreats, and who have encouraged building upon Henri's spirituality, as I have tried to do in this book, rather than just reviewing it. For Michael Ford, who gave us *Wounded Prophet* and contributed so much to the second retreat on Henri that I led. For those who have gathered at Ghost Ranch in New Mexico and Kirkridge in Pennsylvania for retreats I led on Henri's life and writings, whom I fondly remember for their willingness to offer themselves to one another. For churches that have invited me to lead "mini-retreats" on Henri: Oaklands Presbyterian Church in Laurel, Maryland; Fourth Presbyterian Church in Chicago. For many groups that have invited me to speak to them about Henri.

At the end of the first retreat at Ghost Ranch, I sat alone in the meeting room after everyone had left, lights out, candles lit. It is easier for me to comprehend the resurrection because during that weeklong dialogue about Henri among those familiar or who wanted to become familiar with his writings, Henri came alive again. I was privileged to introduce him to people who had never met him in person. As we discussed his writings and viewed videos of him, the sparkle in his eyes, the smile on his face, the vibrancy of his body, the wisdom in his words—all were still there as if he had never left us. Now that the week was over, I cried tears of grief at having to say goodbye once more. And in prayer I thanked Henri.

This is the gift that you, the reader, bring me in wanting to meet Henri through this little book of meditations. You have brought him to life again for me, and I thank you. And I grieve a little having to let it go.

I thank editor George Graham and publisher Timothy Staveteig of Pilgrim Press and the Press itself for wanting to bring you, the readers, this book; for believing in me and my vision of writing meditations on Henri's life; and for George's extremely helpful editorial suggestions. I thank Maureen Wright of the Henri Nouwen Literary Centre for providing encouragement and support, as well as additional books and videos. And I thank the many publishers of Henri's books that I quote for their kind permission to use his words (the list of these follows); my hope is that these excerpts will whet the appetite of readers to find and read the books themselves.

I thank copyeditor Kris Firth for helping me make my thoughts clearer, proofreader Deborah Gallaway for saving us from embarrassing mistakes, cover designer Rick Kuttler and text designer Frederick Porter for the appealing look of the book, and editorial and production director Janice Brown and administrative assistant Monitta Lowe for all of their help. I thank marketing communications associate Aimee Jannsohn and all those involved with the marketing, distribution, and sales of the book, as well as all who review and recommend this book to others.

Lastly but mostly I want to thank God for giving me both life and meaning as well as parents who gave me their faith and their love before God lifted them up.

Chris Glaser

✳

Excerpts from *Adam: God's Beloved* by Henri Nouwen, copyright © 1997 by The Estate of Henri J. M. Nouwen. Used by permission of Orbis Books; Darton, Longman & Todd Ltd. (United Kingdom); and HarperCollinsReligious (Australia).

Excerpts from *Aging: The Fulfillment of Life* by Henri Nouwen and Walter Gaffney, copyright © 1974 by Henri J. M. Nouwen and Walter Gaffney. Used by permission of Doubleday, a division of Random House.

Excerpts from *Angels Over the Net,* a video documentary featuring Henri Nouwen, copyright © 1996 by CB Productions, 1109 S. Main Street, Lindale, Texas 75771. Used by permission of CB Productions.

Excerpts from *Beyond the Mirror: Reflections on Death and Life* by Henri J. M. Nouwen, copyright © 1990 by Henri J. M. Nouwen. All rights reserved. Used by permission of The Crossroad Publishing Company, New York.

Excerpts from *Bread for the Journey: A Daybook of Wisdom and Faith* by Henri J. M. Nouwen, copyright © 1996 by Henri J. M. Nouwen. Reprinted by permission of HarperCollins Publishers Inc. and Darton, Longman & Todd, Ltd. (United Kingdom).

Excerpts from *Can You Drink the Cup?* by Henri J. M. Nouwen. Copyright © 1996 by Ave Maria Press, P.O. Box 428, Notre Dame, IN 46556, www.avemariapress.com. Used with permission of the publisher.

Excerpts from *Clowning in Rome* by Henri Nouwen, copyright © 1979 by Henri J. M. Nouwen. Used by permission of Doubleday, a division of Random House.

Excerpts from *Creative Ministry* by Henri Nouwen, copyright © 1971 by Henri J. M. Nouwen. Used by permission of Doubleday, a division of Random House.

Excerpts from *With Burning Hearts* by Henri Nouwen, copyright © 1994 by Henri J. M. Nouwen. Used by permission of Orbis Books and Claretian Publications (India).

Excerpts from *With Open Hands* by Henri J. M. Nouwen. Copyright © 1995 by Ave Maria Press, P.O. Box 428, Notre Dame, IN 46556, www.avemariapress.com. Used with permission of the publisher.

Excerpts from *The Wounded Healer* by Henri Nouwen, copyright © 1972 by Henri J. M. Nouwen. Used by permission of Doubleday, a division of Random House.

Excerpts from a personal letter to Chris Glaser and Mark King dated February 26, 1996, used by permission of Sue Mosteller, literary executrix of The Estate of Henri J. M. Nouwen.

✳

www.nouwen.net
www.nouwen.org

Henri Nouwen Literary Centre
11339 Yonge Street
Richmond Hill, ON
Canada L4S 1L1

Henri Nouwen Society, U.S.
P.O. Box 230523, Ansonia Station
New York, NY 10023 USA

For information on the L'Arche community or
Daybreak Publications catalogues:
L'Arche Daybreak
11339 Yonge Street
Richmond Hill, ON
Canada L4S 1L1

WORKS BY HENRI J. M. NOUWEN

Adam: God's Beloved. Maryknoll, N.Y.: Orbis, 1997.

Aging: The Fulfillment of Life. Coauthored with Walter Gaffney. New York: Doubleday, 1974.

Beyond the Mirror: Reflections on Death and Life. New York: Crossroad, 1990.

Bread for the Journey: Thoughts for Every Day of the Year. San Francisco: HarperSanFrancisco, 1997.

Can You Drink the Cup? The Challenge of the Spiritual Life. Notre Dame, Ind.: Ave Maria, 1996.

Clowning in Rome: Reflections on Solitude, Celibacy, Prayer and Contemplation. New York: Doubleday Image, 1979.

Compassion: A Reflection on the Christian Life. With Donald P. McNeill and Douglas A. Morrison. New York: Doubleday Image, 1983.

Creative Ministry: Beyond Professionalism in Teaching, Preaching, Counseling, Organizing and Celebrating. New York: Doubleday, 1971.

A Cry for Mercy: Prayers from the Genesee. New York: Doubleday, 1981.

The Genesee Diary: Report from a Trappist Monastery. New York: Doubleday, 1976.

Gracias! A Latin America Journal. San Francisco: Harper & Row, 1983.

Heart Speaks to Heart: Three Prayers to Jesus. Notre Dame, Ind.: Ave Maria, 1989.

Here and Now: Living in the Spirit. New York: Crossroad, 1994.

In Memoriam. Notre Dame, Ind.: Ave Maria, 1980.

In the Name of Jesus: Reflections on Christian Leadership. New York: Crossroad, 1989.

The Inner Voice of Love: A Journey Through Anguish to Freedom. New York: Doubleday, 1996.

Intimacy: Pastoral Psychological Essays. Notre Dame, Ind.: Fides, 1969; San Francisco: Harper & Row, 1981.

A Letter of Consolation. San Francisco: Harper & Row, 1982.

Letters to Marc About Jesus. San Francisco: HarperSanFrancisco, 1988.

Life of the Beloved: Spiritual Living in a Secular World. New York: Crossroad, 1992.

Lifesigns: Intimacy, Fecundity, & Ecstasy in Christian Perspective. New York: Doubleday, 1986.

The Living Reminder: Service and Prayer in Memory of Jesus Christ. New York: Seabury, 1977; San Francisco: HarperSanFrancisco, 1983.

Our Greatest Gift: A Meditation on Dying and Caring. San Francisco: HarperSanFrancisco, 1994.

Out of Solitude: Three Meditations on the Christian Life. Notre Dame, Ind.: Ave Maria, 1974.

The Primacy of the Heart: Cuttings from a Journal. Edited by Lewy Olfson, St. Benedict Center, Box 5070, Madison, WI, 1988, booklet.

Reaching Out: The Three Movements of the Spiritual Life. New York: Doubleday, 1975.

The Return of the Prodigal Son. New York: Doubleday, 1992.

The Road to Daybreak: A Spiritual Journey. New York: Doubleday, 1988.

The Road to Peace. Edited by John Dear. Maryknoll, N.Y.: Orbis, 1998.

Turn My Mourning into Dancing: Finding Hope in Hard Times. Compiled and edited by Timothy Jones. Nashville, Tenn.: W Publishing Group, 2001.

With Burning Hearts: A Meditation on the Eucharistic Life. Maryknoll, N.Y.: Orbis, 1994.

With Open Hands. Notre Dame, Ind.: Ave Maria Press, 1972; New revised edition, 1995.

The Way of the Heart: Desert Spirituality and Contemporary Ministry. New York: Seabury, 1981; San Francisco: HarperSanFrancisco, 1983.

The Wounded Healer: Ministry in Contemporary Society. New York: Doubleday, 1972.

BIOGRAPHIES

Beumer, Jurjen. *Henri Nouwen: A Restless Seeking for God.* New York: Crossroad, 1998.

Ford, Michael. *Wounded Prophet: A Portrait of Henri J. M. Nouwen.* London: Darton, Longman and Todd, 1999; New York: Doubleday, 1999.

AUDIO AND VIDEO

Angels Over the Net. Featuring Henri Nouwen. 30 minutes. CB Productions, 1109 S. Main Street, Lindale, TX 75771. 903/882-0882.

Henri J. M. Nouwen. Presentation of 5 May 1994. L'Arche of Mobile, 151 S. Ann Street, Mobile, Alabama 36604. 205/438-2094.

Henri J. M. Nouwen. Michael Ford audio interview on BBC Radio, 28 August 1992.

Straight to the Heart: The Life of Henri Nouwen. 50 minutes. Windborne Productions, 141 Drakenfield Road, Markham, ON, L3P 1G9 Canada. www.windborneproductions.com.

OTHER REFERENCES

Borg, Marcus. *Meeting Jesus Again for the First Time.* San Francisco: HarperSanFrancisco, 1994.

Campbell, Joseph, with Bill Moyers. *The Power of Myth.* New York: Doubleday, 1988.

Chervin, Ronda De Sola, ed. *Prayers of the Women Mystics.* Ann Arbor, Mich.: Servant Publications, 1992.

Fosdick, Harry Emerson. *The Meaning of Prayer.* New York: Association Press (YMCA), 1915, 1925.

Hillesum, Etty. *An Interrupted Life: The Diaries of Etty Hillesum 1941–43.* New York: Washington Square Press, 1983.

Merton, Thomas. *The Wisdom of the Desert.* New York: New Directions, 1960.

Merton, Thomas. *The Silent Life.* New York: Dell, 1957, 1959.

Miles, Jack. *Christ: A Crisis in the Life of God.* New York: Alfred A. Knopf, 2001.